W9-BKP-320

A
Dialogue on
Comparable Worth

MICHAEL EVAN GOLD

ILR Press
New York State School of
Industrial and Labor Relations
Cornell University

© Copyright 1983 by Cornell University
All rights reserved

Cover design: Kathleen Dalton
Composed by Eastern Graphics
Printed and bound by Braun-Brumfield

ISBN: 0-87546-098-4 (cloth)
ISBN: 0-87546-099-2 (paperback)

Cataloging in Publication Data

Gold, Michael Evan.
   A dialogue on comparable worth.
   Bibliography: p.
   1.   Equal pay for equal work—United States.
I. Title.
HD6061.2.U6G64   1983   331.2′1   83-8508
ISBN 0-87546-098-4
ISBN 0-87546-099-2 (pbk.)

Copies may be ordered from
ILR Press
New York State School of
Industrial and Labor Relations
Cornell University
Ithaca, NY 14853

Second Printing 1984

Printed in the United States of America
5432

I dedicate this book to
Kebbeh Calypso Gold
in the hope that when she comes of age,
the arguments in these pages
will be a matter of history.

Contents

Preface

The moderator, advocate, and critic in this dialogue are products of my imagination, though most of the facts and arguments they present are based on published sources. Readers who wish to refer to the sources on which I have relied will find references in the Notes. These notes contain only sources; all discussion is where it belongs, in the text. Readers who wish to learn more about the issues, but have limited desire to immerse themselves in scholarly literature, may find guidance in the section Some General Readings at the end of the References.

A number of colleagues have been kind enough to read and comment on drafts of this essay. In particular, I thank Alice Cook, Ronald Ehrenberg, George Milkovich, and Olivia Mitchell for their detailed and helpful notes. If I have misunderstood their suggestions, the fault is mine. I also thank Dean Charles Rehmus of the New York State School of Industrial and Labor Relations for providing the research support that prompted this work.

A
Dialogue on
Comparable Worth

MODERATOR   Comparable worth is the EEO issue of the decade. The purpose of this dialogue is to present both, or at least two, sides of the debate over comparable worth. In essence, it raises the question of whether women are underpaid for their work. Secretaries, for example, earn less than plumbers, and social workers earn less than stockbrokers. Is it mere coincidence that most secretaries and social workers are women, while most plumbers and stockbrokers are men? For the sake of convenience, the participants in this dialogue have agreed that jobs held predominantly by women may be referred to as "women's jobs" or "women's work" and jobs held predominantly by men may be referred to as "men's jobs" or "men's work" and that our use of these terms is not sexist because it is descriptive, not normative. We accept the definition of *predominantly* used by the Women's Bureau of the U.S. Department of Labor, that is, 70 percent or more of the occupants of a job or occupation are of the same sex.[1] So the question becomes, Is it coincidence that women's jobs generally pay less than men's jobs?

It is important to point out that the issue of comparable

worth is distinct from the issue of equal pay for equal work. The latter issue contemplates that men and women perform the same work, and the question is simply whether they ought to be paid the same for it. Comparable worth, on the other hand, contemplates that men and women are performing different work. Two questions arise: Is the women's work as valuable to the employer as the men's work? If so, should the women be paid as much as the men? For example, nurses are paid less than trash collectors. Is the work of nurses undervalued and underpaid? Should the pay of nurses be raised? If so, how much?

The debate has taken shape along the following lines. First, it is noted that, on average, women earn sixty cents for every dollar men earn. Why does this "earnings gap" exist? Without anticipating the arguments our participants will present, I can say that advocates of comparable worth claim the gap exists because of sex discrimination, for example, the exclusion of women from high-paying jobs. Critics of comparable worth attribute the gap to legitimate causes such as differences in men's and women's job-related characteristics and tastes. Advocates rely on studies that suggest that women are paid less by employers than men would be paid for the same work. Critics question the validity of these studies.

Second comes the question of how to determine the value of a specific job. Advocates of comparable worth argue that job evaluation, if purged of certain deficiencies, can establish the value of jobs. Critics are generally more positive about job evaluation in its present form, but still favor allowing the labor market to assign prices to jobs.

Third, advocates and critics disagree about the economic consequences of using job evaluation to raise the pay of women's jobs. Critics predict inefficiency, misallocation of resources, and eventual government control of the price and supply of labor. Advocates are more hopeful.

Fourth, we reach the legal issues. Did Congress intend the Equal Pay Act of 1963 or Title VII of the Civil Rights Act of 1964 to support a cause of action for sex discrimination based on comparisons of the value of jobs to an employer?[2] Are courts likely to order increases in the pay of women's jobs under the aegis of either of these statutes? Advocates answer yes and yes; critics answer no and no.

Finally, there is the role of the labor movement. Will unions bring comparable worth to the bargaining table and improve the pay of women's work through collective bargaining? Advocates think unions have already begun to do it, and critics have their doubts.

I will now turn the debate over to the participants.

ADVOCATE   Let us begin at the beginning. I quote from Leviticus.

And the Lord spoke unto Moses, saying, Speak unto the children of Israel, and say unto them:

When a man shall clearly utter a vow of persons unto the Lord, according to thy valuation, then thy valuation for the male from twenty years old even unto sixty years old, even thy valuation shall be fifty shekels of silver, after the shekel of the sanctuary. And if it be a female, then thy valuation shall be thirty shekels. (Lev. 27:1–4)

Little has changed over the millennia. The average female, white, full-time worker in America earns only 56 percent as much as the average male, white, full-time worker.[3] In fact, this earnings gap is greater now than it was several years ago. In 1955 the average white woman earned 65 percent as much as the average white man, so you can see the relative earnings of women have declined, not increased, in recent years.[4] It is astounding that the mean earnings of female college graduates are lower than the mean earnings of white men with an eighth-grade education.[5] What makes these facts even more outrageous—and constitutes a true index of the extent of discrimination against women—is that the earnings of almost every category of minority men have improved vis-à-vis white men in recent years. Men are moving ahead, and women are falling behind!

CRITIC   I must interject here that national averages conceal more than they reveal. There is a host of variables that affect earnings and that vary across racial and sexual classes. Some of the most important of these variables are occupation, experience, and hours worked. If men and women prepare for and hold different jobs, keep them for different lengths of time, and work at them for different numbers of hours per week, no one should be surprised if average earnings were different. That 56 percent or 60 percent statistic is very nearly a conscious lie.

ADVOCATE   You should be more careful of whom you accuse of nearly lying. The U.S. Civil Rights Commission has used multiple regression analysis to take account of all the variables you mentioned and then some. Adjusting for occupational prestige (with which income should correlate positively), education, weeks and hours worked, average income in state of residence, and age (which captures some, though not all, of the experience factor), the commission found that white women earned 57 percent as much as white men in 1959, 54 percent as much in 1969, and 57 percent as much in 1975. In contrast, the adjusted figures for black men show real gains. In 1959 black men earned 71 percent as much as white men, in 1969, 75 percent, and in 1975, 85 percent.[6] So the conclusion I drew earlier is correct, even when appropriate adjustments are made: men are moving ahead, and women are falling behind.

CRITIC   I am not sure that occupational prestige is a good proxy for income. A truck driver can earn more than a college professor, though the professor enjoys more prestige than the driver. In fact, for many people prestige is a substitute for dollars.

As for the relationship of age to experience, I seriously doubt the former captures much of the latter. Suppose, for example, a woman takes a job after rearing a family. Let us say she is forty years old and worked five years before leaving the labor market to rear a family. A forty-year-old man who has worked steadily may have twenty years of experience behind him. Ten years later, the woman has fifteen years of experience, but the man now has thirty years. So he is still fifteen years ahead of her, and she will never catch up with him.

Experience is important in another way. A major reason that women's average earnings have declined relative to men's in the past twenty years is that, today, the average male worker is more experienced and has more seniority, compared to the average female worker, than was the case twenty years ago. Why? You know the reasons. Women have been flocking to the labor market. It is more acceptable today than it was twenty or thirty years ago for married women and mothers to hold jobs; women's liberation and economic necessity have contributed to this change in attitude. In the 1970s birth rates fell, and divorce rates rose, both sharply. Again, more women were looking for jobs. Now, if the population had been in a steady state while attitudes and behavior changed, there would have been some increase in women's participation in the labor market. But it happened that these changes occurred at the same time the children of the post–World War II baby boom were growing up, becoming educated, and entering the labor market. So the statistics are dramatic. Half of all women are now members of the labor force, an increase of 50 percent since 1950. And 42 percent of all workers are now female, an increase of 46 percent since 1950. Most of these additional female workers are under age thirty-five; the greatest increase has been for women between 25 and 34.[7] In other words, the labor market has been flooded with young women, who have simply dragged down the average experience and seniority of all working women. Because experience and compensation are correlated, it follows that the average working woman today earns less than she did twenty years ago when compared with the average man. Of course, if these women stay in the labor market, their average experience will rise relative to men's, and the women will begin to catch up. But it will take time.

ADVOCATE   You conveniently ignore a critical fact: occupational segregation. More women than ever before may be working, but they are working in low-paying, dead-end jobs. The earnings curve of men rises steadily over their lifetimes. The earnings curve of women is virtually flat.[8] In other words, women are doing women's work, as they always have, and they are underpaid for it. Women are much more likely to work in the clerical and service occupations, and men are much more likely to work in the craft and laboring occupations.[9] The 1970 census listed 553 occupations: 310 had 80 percent or more male incumbents, and 50 had 80 percent or more female incumbents. Overall, 70 percent of the male workers and 54 percent of the female workers were concentrated in occupations dominated by their own sex.[10] In fact, one-fourth of the women held jobs that were at least 95 percent female.[11] And despite what you may say about changing attitudes and behavior, these facts have not changed over time. Indeed, occupational segregation has been getting worse. Between 1940 and 1970, the number of occupations with 70 percent or more men or women rose.[12]

Naturally, the men's jobs pay better than the women's jobs. In fact, the more women who work in an occupation, the less it is paid. A study based on 1970 census data showed that each additional percentage point of women in an occupation resulted in a drop in median compensation for that occupation of forty-two dollars a year. Jobs with no female occupants paid double what jobs with no male occupants paid. And analysis shows that sex is the cause of the difference. When predictions of median earnings were based on seven variables (including schooling, experience in the labor force, job requirements, and sex), the six variables other than sex had almost no effect on the outcomes; but the sex composition of occupations nearly replicated the ratio of male income to female income.[13] Other studies have shown that more than 70 percent of the earnings gap is attributable to the sex of the incumbents.[14]

Not only do men and women work in different occupations, but also men and women work in different jobs within the same occupation. That is, even if an occupation is integrated by sex, there may be job segregation within the occupation. For example, in the clerical occupations, 92 percent of all letter carriers were men, while 93 percent of stenographers were women. In the craft occupations, 98 percent of construction workers were men, while most bookbinders, decorators, and window dressers were women.[15] Job segregation costs women money, just as occupational segregation does. A 1971 study by the Bureau of Labor Statistics showed that men had 18 percent higher earnings than women in the occupations examined. For these same occupations, the male advantage fell to 11 percent in firms that employed both men and women, but rose to 22 percent in firms that were totally segregated by sex.[16]

CRITIC   I agree, as one must, that men and women tend to work in different occupations. But I am uncomfortable with the term *occupational segregation* because segregation implies there is something wrong with the practice. In fact, however, there is nothing wrong with *occupational concentration* because in most cases the men and women have freely chosen the jobs they hold. No one in this country can force a man to be a nurse or a woman to be a stockbroker.

The process begins in school. Boys and girls take courses and acquire knowledge and skill that are valuable, or not valuable, in the labor market. In a sense, children in school are investing in themselves. Instead of working, they are building up a store of *human capital.* Eventually, the quality and quantity of their human capital will affect their abilities to earn money.

A substantial portion of the earnings gap can be attributed to the different qualities and quantities of human capital acquired by boys and girls before they enter the labor market. Few boys, but many girls, expect to become homemakers. Later in life, such a girl might decide to take a job—perhaps her children have left home; perhaps her spouse has died or been divorced. Her investment in homemaking skills will not pay off in the labor market. She will generally be limited to relatively unskilled, low-paying jobs. Her situation may be unfortunate, but it is the result of her own choice. Boys, on the other hand, typically acquire marketable skills.

Of course, not all girls elect home economics and sewing courses. Some girls prepare for jobs. But here again, girls may freely choose to prepare for different jobs than boys prepare for. Girls more than boys prepare for jobs helping disadvantaged people, such as social worker. Girls more than boys prepare for jobs working with children, such as elementary school teacher and child care worker. Girls more than boys prepare for jobs whose duties tend not to change over time, such as librarian, and for jobs that are easy to enter and leave, such as dental technician. Finally, I think that girls more than boys choose jobs that are personally satisfying to perform. It happens that none of these jobs commands a high rate of pay in the market.[17]

ADVOCATE   I will concede that human capital affects earnings and that boys seem to acquire more human capital than girls. I will also concede that more women than men are social workers, elementary school teachers, and librarians. But I will not concede that women freely choose to invest less in themselves and freely choose to take low-paying jobs. The truth is that girls are forced into it. Either they are socialized into believing they should be subservient to men, or they are discriminatorily excluded from valuable training programs.[18] Some girls are excluded from vocational education programs, or are steered away from them by school counselors, or are pressured by family and peers into other programs. But most girls are simply brainwashed, and they are brainwashed so effectively that they exclude themselves, despite their natural talents. Brainwashing begins when girls are so young that they do not even realize what has happened to them. It is no accident that little boys play cowboy and doctor and little girls play mother and nurse; that big boys compete in baseball and football and big girls talk about boys or help around the house; and that men take good jobs and women take menial jobs. If women choose low-paying jobs, the reason is a sexist process of socialization, which teaches girls that a woman's place is in the home.

CRITIC   Do you have empirical evidence that girls are socialized against their will?

ADVOCATE   No, but I do have evidence that women receive a lesser return on their human capital investments than men, and that means women are being discriminated against.[19] Do you have empirical evidence that women prefer personally satisfying but low-paying jobs?

CRITIC   No, but I do have reason to believe that women are not actually forced into the jobs they take. In fact, preparing for relatively low-paying jobs is a perfectly rational choice for many women. Suppose a girl in high school expects to work a few years, then become a homemaker for the rest of her life. If she is thinking about going to college, she may realize she would be better off spending those years earning money instead of paying money to go to school. In addition, she will realize she wants a job she can perform immediately upon leaving high school. She has no incentive to forgo present income for apprenticeship or on-the-job training because she does not expect to be in the labor market long enough to capitalize on the training. And she will also realize that her best bet is a job that pays beginners about as much as experienced workers—no long ladders of promotion for this woman. But suppose this woman wants to go to college. Would she not be wise to take courses that will enrich her personal life more than her pocketbook? In either case, she will be unlikely to earn a high income from her jobs, but she may earn as much as possible in the short time she works.

Suppose another woman expects to work a while, leave the labor force for a number of years while her children are growing up (or at least until the youngest enters school), and then return to work. She too might pass up a chance to go to college, preferring a job that provides immediate income. She would also be wise to acquire skills that would not atrophy or become obsolete while she stays at home.

Such skills might not be highly compensated, but they would still be valuable to her when she returned to work. If she took the chance to go to college, she certainly would have to think hard about enrolling in an expensive postgraduate curriculum leading to a professional career.

Each of these girls, if she is rational in thinking about her future, will realize something else: because her husband will probably be permanently attached to the labor force, he will earn more than she will. As a result, if he gets an opportunity to advance his career by taking a job in another community, family income will be maximized by making the move. Knowing this, the woman will prepare herself for jobs that are easy to enter and exit. Such jobs may not be high-paying, but they will be available after a move.

So far I have been talking about entering the labor market. I have argued a girl's expectations about her future could influence her rationally to prepare for some jobs as opposed to others. I want to finish the argument by mentioning briefly some rational decisions a woman could make in the labor market itself—decisions that maximize the family's income, or at least the family's happiness, but not the woman's pay. Let us assume both husband and wife are working or want to work. Probably the man can earn more money than the woman, for the reasons I have just mentioned. Now suppose there are children. In most cases, one spouse or the other must assume primary responsibility for sending the children to school in the morning, for taking off from work when they are sick, and for being at home at night and on weekends. It makes economic sense for the woman to assume this responsibility because her working hours generate less income than the man's. As a result, many women rationally limit themselves to jobs that are close to home, have convenient hours, offer generous leave allowances, and do not require overtime or travel. Now suppose this woman is offered a good job—say, a promotion—in another community. She could accept the job and live apart from her husband, and that would truly maximize the family's income. But I think most families would decide that staying together is worth more than the extra income the woman could earn. Another possibility is that the woman could accept the job and the husband could take his chances on finding work in the new community. Again, I think most families would reject this option because of the possibility the husband will not find as good a job, meaning that family income might decrease, and because of the certainty that the husband will not be drawing a paycheck for a period of time. On the other hand, if the husband is offered a promotion, most families would make the move. Even though the wife may not earn as much because she must sacrifice her seniority and may not find as good a job in the new community, the chances are that the husband's raise will more than offset the wife's loss. So family income is maximized, though the woman's pay decreases. Of course, there is the certainty that the wife will be out of work until she finds a new job, but the husband's income may well be enough to live on while the wife hunts for work.

Another effect becomes important here. By limiting themselves to jobs that are close to home, easy to enter and exit, and require skills that do not depreciate, women become concentrated in a narrower range of occupations than men. With so many women pursuing so few jobs, competition naturally reduces the price of women's labor. Economists call this phenomenon *crowding*.[20]

I realize the breadth of the argument I have just made, and I admit I cannot support all of it with empirical evidence. But I can report two very interesting sets of data. First, the Bureau of Labor Statistics recently published the 1981 figures on median weekly wages and salaries of full-time workers. In families in which husbands and wives both worked, the average wife earned $230. Because the average husband in such a family earned more—$387—it is reasonable to suppose that most of the wives were taking primary responsibility for any children. In families in which a woman alone was the provider, the average woman earned $232, which is almost exactly the same as earned by the average wife whose husband worked. I think we can safely assume that most women who were the sole providers for their families took primary responsibility for any children. (The slightly lower pay of the women living with their husbands may be attributable to the slightly greater likelihood that these women will have children as compared to women without spouses present.) Now comes the interesting comparison. Other women—that is, unmarried women without children—earned on average $248, or about 7 percent more than the first two classes of women.[21] I believe this difference is probably close to the portion of the earnings gap that is attributable to child-rearing responsibilities.

The other interesting data are the salary offers made in 1976 to bachelor degree candidates. The National Science Foundation reported average offers made to candidates who had studied in nineteen different curricula across the fields of business, science, engineering, humanities, and social science. Men had higher starting offers in ten curricula, women in nine, and the average woman's offer was 99.2 percent of the average man's.[22] Two conclusions, which I admit need further testing, can be drawn from these data. The first is that there was no labor market discrimination against female college graduates. This result does not surprise me, for it is irrational for an employer to discriminate against qualified people.

The second conclusion follows from the first. Because it has always been irrational for an employer to hire a man instead of a better qualified woman, the major change has not been employers' behavior, but women's behavior. Women being graduated from college in 1976 probably entered high school in 1968 or 1969, well after Title VII was in force and the women's liberation movement was in gear. These women—certainly those who went to college and looked for jobs afterwards—accumulated the same quality and quantity of human capital as the men with whom they competed for jobs. With the same human capital, the women got the same opportunities. I will be interested to see where these women stand in comparison to the male members of their age group twenty years from now.

My point, in sum, is that some women's expectations about their future have led them rationally to limit their self-investment, and that limitation has resulted in women's holding lower paying jobs than men on average and to flat earnings curves. When men and women have the same expectations about their future, as seems to be true of recent college graduates, women invest in themselves to the same degree as men and reap the same return on their investment.

ADVOCATE   I am pleased our critic concedes the fact of occupational segregation—

CRITIC   I concede only the fact of occupational concentration.

ADVOCATE   —and I certainly agree that women are crowded in a narrow range of occupations. But I think there are much more believable causes of crowding than the rationality hypothesis our critic suggests. Before I mention them, however, I want to point out how tightly our critic's arguments fit together. Girls expect to become homemakers, so they do not acquire marketable skills. Lacking skills, women take low-paying jobs. When women become mothers, they maximize family income by accepting low-paying jobs with convenient hours close to home and by following their husbands from town to town. After the children leave home, women remain confined to low-paying jobs because of lack of skill and experience. In the meantime, girls who are growing up observe all this and, realizing they too will become homemakers and mothers, do not acquire marketable skills, take low-paying jobs—and so on. It is a self-perpetuating system that locks women into menial jobs. It is a vicious circle as well. Women stay home because of low wages; women earn low wages because they stay at home. Unless we do something to break into this circle, it will roll on forever.

Now let me offer more realistic explanations of crowding than our critic's rationality theory. In the first place, sexist socialization does not stop in school. If a couple decided the woman ought to work and the man ought to stay home with the children, society would come down on them as hard as it does on racially mixed marriages. In the second place, there is nothing rational about a woman's taking a low-paying job if she can get a high-paying one. A woman takes a low-paying job because society excludes her from high-paying jobs. Average people do not have anything like the range of choices open to them that economists assume. We take the chances that come our way, and women are denied many chances that men are afforded. In other words, a woman does not have the same opportunity as a man to build up her human capital.

Before Title VII took effect, it was legal in most states for an employer to refuse to hire a woman, or to hire a woman but assign her to a menial job, or to assign a woman to a good job but refuse to promote her, for no better reason than her sex. Even today, Title VII does not prohibit an employer with fewer than fifteen employees from discriminating against women.[23] And many employers with fifteen or more employees continue to discriminate against women by excluding them from the best jobs, as the court cases show. Some colleges, for example, have been loath to appoint women to professorships, or have appointed but paid them less than men, and some cities and counties have been unwilling to employ women as fire fighters or patrol officers. Women commonly have been limited to certain jobs in factories.[24] In fact, so-called protective legislation in every state excluded women from work they were fully capable of performing.[25] Some employers have used one set of criteria for hiring men and another, more stringent set of criteria for hiring women. For example, in one case an employer would hire any qualified man, regardless of the ages of his children, but refused to hire a qualified woman if she had a pre-school-age child.[26] In another case, an employer discharged any woman as soon as she married, and another employer discharged any woman as soon as she became pregnant.[27] Many employers have simply assumed that a particular job was too difficult for any woman to perform.[28] And many employers have utilized hiring standards that, although neutral on the face, excluded more qualified women than men and were not related to successful job performance. For example, prison guards in Alabama had to stand at least five feet two inches tall and weigh at least one hundred twenty pounds. This standard did not openly distinguish between men and women, yet in application it excluded 41 percent of the female population but less than 1 percent of the male population. When the standard was challenged, the state failed to prove any correlation between satisfying the standard and performing successfully on the job.[29]

I should add that unions played their role as well. They refused to admit women to membership or to enroll them in apprenticeship programs. Unions also negotiated collective bargaining agreements that reserved the best jobs for men and relegated women to low-paying jobs with no chance for advancement.[30]

There is other evidence that women are excluded from the best jobs. Social scientists have been allowed to examine the practices of some large corporations. The scholars found that, of men and women with equal qualifications, the men were likely to be assigned to the more responsible, better paying jobs that provided greater opportunities for promotion.[31] In another study of retail sales clerks, researchers observed that men were more likely than women to be selected to sell expensive items like furniture and major appliances.[32]

CRITIC   I do not deny that individual employers used to, and some may continue to, exclude women from jobs. A handful of court cases and a couple of case studies, however, are hardly conclusive as to the practice of America's 14 million private firms. I am much more influenced by economic theory, which clearly shows that, if women are as productive as men, employers who discriminate against women will suffer in the marketplace—in other words, that employers have a real reason not to discriminate. The reason is quite simple. Some employers are certainly free of prejudice or greedy enough to ignore their prejudices. If other employers are discriminating against productive women, these unprejudiced or greedy employers will be able to hire women at bargain rates and, with this competitive advantage, drive their discriminatory competitors out of business. A rational employer will realize that discrimination is costly and will refrain from it. An irrational employer will not be around very long.[33]

ADVOCATE   The problem with our critic's argument is that it relies on a false model of the labor market. That model assumes that employers compete with one another for qualified workers and that workers compete with one another for jobs. The competitive, or neoclassical, model may be true for white men, but it is not true for women—or blacks or other minorities, for that matter. The correct model for women and minorities is the dual, or stratified, labor market, and it reflects a phenomenon called labor market segmentation.

In the competitive model of the labor market, the wage rate of a job is the result of the forces of supply and demand. This model assumes that workers have information about job opportunities and access to those opportunities; otherwise, the supply of labor cannot respond to the demand for it. But if information about job opportunities is suppressed, or if access to jobs is denied, wage rates would not reflect the intersections of supply and demand curves. Most of the time, information about and access to the highest paying jobs are limited to men. When this happens, employers can pay women much less than their true value to the firm, and the women—who do not know about better jobs or who lack the skills for better jobs because of exclusion from training programs—are not wooed away by hypothetical non-discriminatory employers. The result is that the market cannot punish discriminatory employers, despite what economic theory dictates.[34]

How are information and access denied to women? I have already argued that women are socialized into preparing for low-paying jobs and that women are excluded from other jobs and from training programs. Once this pattern is in place, we have a dual labor market—one for men's jobs, the other for women's jobs. For example, how many female apprentices do you know, and how many male secretaries do you know? Men and women may compete with members of their own sex, but not with members of the opposite sex.[35] So when Sir Galahad rides up on his white horse and opens his nondiscriminatory business, he finds only men at the hiring window.

CRITIC   Which means the answer is simple: enforce existing laws against sex discrimination in jobs and apprenticeship programs. When women have skills, they will get good jobs, and that will be the end of the dual labor market.

ADVOCATE   I am afraid it is not that simple, and one of the causes of my fear is an institution called the internal labor market.[36] Many employers seek to fill job openings from within the firm. Jobs are designed to provide on-the-job training, and they are clustered to create ladders of promotion. In such firms, therefore, only entry-level jobs are truly part of the labor market. Wages for entry-level jobs may respond to supply and demand forces, but internal promotions are largely immune to those forces because the only demand comes from within the firm and the only supply is current employees.[37] Wages in an internal market are not likely to fall below wages for comparable jobs outside the firm because employees would leave the firm. In fact, wages in an internal market tend to be higher than wages elsewhere because internal markets are concentrated in large firms in industries with advanced technology, large capital investment, and high profits, and the jobs in these firms require a great deal of human capital investment. These firms compose the primary segment of the economy and employ about 40 percent of the labor force. The primary segment probably corresponds closely to what John Kenneth Galbraith called the planning system.[38] Such firms can afford to pay high wages because of their high profits and, sometimes, because of their ability to pass on wage costs to customers.

Data show that employees in the primary segment are paid 25 to 40 percent more than other workers. Needless to add, most employees in the primary segment of the economy are men.[39]

If we were to follow our critic's advice—that is, if we did nothing more than enforce existing laws and guarantee women access to jobs and training programs—we would wait a long time to see any progress. In the first place, the only women who would benefit from this remedy would be recent entrants into the labor market.[40] All the rest of the more than 40 million women in the labor force would be left out for any of several reasons.

Consider a typical woman who has been a secretary with the same employer for a few years. When an entry-level job in a primary segment firm becomes available, she will probably never know of it. If she learns about it, she will probably not qualify for it because she was denied the opportunity to acquire the appropriate skills when she was younger. If she has the appropriate skills, she will probably not get the job because many, mostly younger applicants will compete with her for it. And if she is offered the job, she may have to refuse it because it probably pays less than her present job and offers less job security, and her chances for advancement (given the limited number of promotional opportunities in the typical pyramidal organization) are uncertain.[41] This woman and the millions of women she represents are the victims of sex discrimination, and they deserve a remedy for it.

In the second place, I seriously doubt that the young woman who gets an entry-level job in a primary segment firm will be sailing on oiled waters. She will have to fight for fairness in promotions, leaves of absence, and all the other aspects of employment. If she has to bludgeon her way into a firm in the first place, she can hardly expect a friendly reception.

CRITIC   Even accepting—though I do not—our advocate's thesis about the dual labor market, I continue to believe that my proposal that we enforce existing antidiscrimination laws would work. As before, my reason is simple economic theory. A primary segment employer who hires and promotes women fairly will have an advantage over his competitor who does not promote women. In fact, I suspect that an employer with an internal labor market would create chaos if the firm refused to promote women.

Suppose such an employer has ten—or a hundred or a thousand—entry-level jobs. Let's say one is held by a woman, and the other nine or ninety-nine are held by men. It is time for a promotion. If the woman is the best qualified but the employer discriminates against her and chooses a man, the firm loses a degree of productivity. More central to my immediate point, the firm takes a step toward chaos because the promotee must be replaced. The replacement may be a man or a woman, but eventually—with nondiscriminatory hiring but discriminatory promoting—all those entry-level jobs will be held by women. And if the employer still refuses to promote a woman, the firm is going to be unable to fill his higher level jobs. So even the worst employer will come around in time. It is just not in the employer's economic interest to discriminate.

ADVOCATE   I doubt there is time enough before Armageddon for me to expose all the flaws in our critic's last argument. I will mention only the most obvious. First, if the internal supply pipe became clogged with women, the employer could easily bring in new men. Second, the employer could keep the pipe open for men by promoting a woman once in a while, then hiring a man into the entry-level job and slipping him past the woman who was promoted. Third, why should women who are being discriminated against be asked to wait until internal chaos forces an employer to cease discriminating?

But most important of all, I want to refute our critic's basic argument that employers will come around to fairness because discrimination is not in their best interests. I think it is very much in employers' interests to discriminate against women—or at least employers may think it is—and they will act accordingly. First I will discuss employers who lose profit by discriminating but gain more in other ways. Then I will discuss employers who actually do profit from their discrimination.

To understand why employers benefit from discrimination, we have to know why employers discriminate in the first place. Some employers are simply prejudiced against women. I do not mean that these employers are misogynists, though some probably are. I mean they, like generations of women, have been socialized to believe it is unseemly for a woman to practice law, or it is inappropriate for a woman to build bridges, or it is unthinkable for a woman to supervise a man. Employers may also still believe that men work to support families, while women work only to support themselves or to supplement their husbands' income.

How do prejudiced employers benefit from discrimination? Are they not losing profits by not hiring productive female workers? The benefit comes in the satisfaction of the taste these employers have for discrimination. They are willing to exchange some profits for the pleasure of a rightly ordered world.[42]

Other employers are prejudiced, not so much against any individual woman, as against women in general. These employers believe in and act upon stereotypes, such as that women as a class are less productive than men. If such an employer is a typical primary segment employer who has to invest in training an employee and believes that women on average are absent from work more often than men—or

statistical discrimination

are less willing to work overtime or to travel, have poorer work habits, or are more likely to quit—this employer will be reluctant to hire a woman. The reluctance will be especially strong if criteria other than sex are not helpful in distinguishing better from worse applicants. This employer may not hire women at all or, if the firm does hire them, may limit them to jobs in which turnover costs are minimal—jobs that provide little on-the-job training, offer limited upward mobility, and pay poorly. These attributes characterize jobs in the secondary segment of the economy, into which women are crowded.[43] If the primary segment employer is wrong about women—as the evidence seems to show—the firm is acting against its own best interests.[44] But so long as the employer continues to believe that women are less productive than men, the firm will continue to discriminate.

And it is discrimination, no matter what some people may say, because judging an individual by the characteristics of a class is unjust. Even if women on average are absent more often than men, many individual women are absent less than, or no more often than, many individual men. These women are wrongly penalized. The Supreme Court held just this in *Phillips* v. *Martin Marietta,* the case I mentioned earlier in which an employer was found to have violated Title VII for refusing to hire women with pre-school-age children but freely hiring men with pre-school-age children.[45] The employer believed, perhaps rightly, that such women would work fewer days on average than men, but the Supreme Court effectively required the employer to evaluate applicants and employees as individuals. The Court explicitly came to the same conclusion in a compensation case, *City of Los Angeles* v. *Manhart.*[46] This employer charged female employees a higher rate of contribution to a pension fund, and thus provided them less take-home pay, than their male counterparts. The employer argued that the average woman outlives the average man, but the Court said the law *but are treated as members of other classes, e.g. class of workers.*

requires that employees be treated as individuals, not as members of sexual or racial classes.

Let me mention briefly two mechanisms that protect and preserve the status quo. First, it may be argued that at least the mistaken employer will one day realize that some women are as productive as men and will change attitudes. However, if women are assigned to low-paying, low-productivity jobs, often the women's extra ability will not affect job performance, so the employer will never learn of their ability. If extra ability does enhance job performance, the employer will likely consider the woman to be an exception that proves the rule.[47] Second, it is possible that unprejudiced, well-informed employers could drive their Neanderthal competitors out of business if women were readily available. But when prejudice and mistaken beliefs about women are held widely in a community, the result is that women are not trained properly to hold men's jobs; instead, women are crowded into secondary segment jobs. Even if prejudice and mistaken beliefs are beginning to die out, the dual labor market will continue to operate for a long time to prevent new employers from taking advantage of productive female labor.

Now let us turn to employers who profit from discrimination. Some of these employers may be unprejudiced themselves, but find their employees or customers are prejudiced. Co-workers could refuse to accept a woman in a job. Customers could take their trade to a firm with a man in the job. These groups can exert tremendous pressure on an employer. Indeed, some people think only government-mandated affirmative action can overcome this sort of pressure. At any rate, an employer confronted with employee and customer prejudice may well have no choice but to discriminate if the firm is to stay in business. Thus, when employees or customers are prejudiced, discrimination will be profitable for an employer.

Finally, some employers discriminate because they know women are as good as or better than men. If a ruling class of people in a society can subjugate another class of people and, by exercise of political, economic, and social power, compel members of the subjugated class to work for less compensation than they would earn in a free society, the ruling class can enrich itself.[48] Slavery is proof of this argument. A slave is like an animal: its owner seeks the optimal balance between the cost of maintaining the animal and the benefit of its labor. Feed a mule too little, and it will not be able to work hard enough. Feed a mule too much, and it will eat up profits. At the optimum, and perhaps even some distance from the optimum, an animal creates more profit than a human being, and a slave creates more profit than a hired hand. We know this is true because if the hired hand were cheaper than the slave, the master would soon rid himself of slaves. Thus, the profit motive can lead to discrimination against women, just as prejudice and mistaken generalizations can. Indeed, the profit motive may be the most insidious of all. The prejudiced person truly believes that the people against whom he is prejudiced are inferior; he excludes them from some jobs and pays them less for others because he believes such people are incompetent and unproductive. But the profit maximizer benefits to the extent that his victims' productivity exceeds their compensation. The more productive the victims are, the more the ruling class profits. A profit maximizer has reason to subjugate people he knows to be able, not inferior. A radical feminist might well argue this observation explains why women—our greatest untapped natural resource—were not liberated until a century after blacks were emancipated.

So contrary to what our critic has said, opening entry-level jobs in primary segment firms will not end discrimination against women. Prejudiced employers will still refuse to promote women, and erroneous generalizations about the productivity of women workers will still interfere with their progress. The dual labor market will protect these employers from competitive pressure for a long time to come. And prejudiced employees and customers will still pressure unprejudiced employers into discriminating, and the cynical profit maximizer will still enrich himself by underpaying women. And even if these predictions are wrong, opening entry-level jobs might help recent high school and college graduates, but will do nothing for the woman who has been chained to a typewriter for thirty years and underpaid every day of them.

CRITIC   What is your evidence that women are underpaid? Although I did not agree with it, I understood your argument that the dual labor market would impede the profit maximizer from hiring women at bargain rates and driving his discriminatory competitors out of business. But now you are claiming something else, that a profit maximizer can actually profit from discrimination by underpaying women. I see the method in this madness because comparable worth, after all, is a claim that women should be paid more for the work they do. But even if women were segregated or socialized into low-paying jobs, that would not be proof that women are underpaid in those jobs. And so I ask again, what is the proof of underpayment?

ADVOCATE   Underpayment can occur in two ways. When men and women perform the same jobs, an employer can pay the women less than the men. When men and women perform different jobs, an employer can pay the women less for their job than he would pay men to do that job.

Employers today probably do not frequently pay

women less than men for exactly the same job.[49] The Equal Pay Act is widely understood, and it prohibits this practice. So I think few employers pay a female machine operator less than a male machine operator, unless the differential is justifiable on grounds of merit or seniority. But this is not to say that employers are obeying the Equal Pay Act. They are just more subtle about violating it. The typical case is the employer who assigns different titles to predominately male and predominately female jobs and pays the men more than the women, although the contents of the two jobs are really identical. (The same practice is true for blacks and whites.)[50] Everyone knows that men are called chefs, while women are called cooks. Men are called maitre d's and women hostesses. Men are administrative assistants, women are secretaries. A very common example is a hospital that pays male orderlies more than female nurse's aides, though the jobs are indistinguishable except for who puts the catheter in whom.[51]

CRITIC   Some employers surely do pay women less than men by fabricating different job titles for substantially equal work, and the court cases prove it. But the court cases also prove women think this happens more often than it actually does. I mean that women win some Equal Pay Act cases, but lose at least as many, if not more. For example, many employers distinguish between light and heavy janitorial work. The heavy duty workers are called custodians; the light duty workers are called cleaners. The custodians are paid more than the cleaners. Even though the employers are perfectly willing to hire female custodians and even though women freely choose the lighter duties involved in the cleaner's position, lawsuits are filed—and lost. For example, in *Usery* v. *Columbia University,* the court held the differences between light and heavy cleaning were genuine.[52] So I think a student should take care before generalizing from a few Equal Pay Act cases.

ADVOCATE   I am not generalizing from a few cases. The thousands and hundreds of thousands of Equal Pay Act violations cumulate into national averages. The Bureau of the Census reported in 1973 that female household workers earned only 70 percent as much as men in the same occupation; female clerical workers earned only 66 percent as much as men; female craft workers, 60 percent as much as men; and female managers and administrators, 58 percent as much. These statistics were adjusted for the number of hours worked during the year.[53] Clearly, the Equal Pay Act is widely violated.

An even greater problem, and the one comparable worth is aimed at, is the employer who pays a woman less to do a job than the employer would pay a man to do the job: in other words, underpaying women's work. Evidence of underpayment comes from a variety of sources. One is the connection between occupational segregation and underpayment. Women are believed to be less productive than men, therefore, top-notch, high-paying employers prefer male employees, leaving similarly qualified female employees to jobs in lower paying firms.[54] Other employers place women in low-productivity jobs, which by definition do not pay well (even though they may pay their marginal product).[55]

Let us take the Columbia University case as an example. A pay differential between men's and women's jobs is often defended on the ground that the men do heavier work and are paid a premium for it. Women are less productive in the sense that they cannot do heavy work, so they are paid less. But is heavy work truly more valuable than other work? In the South, heavy, dirty jobs have long been blacks' jobs, and these are the lowest paying, lowest prestige jobs.[56] Clearly, the pay and prestige of a job are related more to who does it than to what is done. Also, we know that, when an occupation loses status and, in consequence, loses ability to command high compensation, the job is opened to women—for example, lawyers in the Soviet Union and bank tellers in America.[57] And, as I mentioned earlier, employers who hire women for a job pay them less than employers who hire men for the same job. Within occupations that are integrated by sex, men and women are not randomly distributed among firms. Firms that hire more men than sex-blind hiring would predict pay better than firms that hire more women. This pattern is consistent across occupations and labor markets, confirming the link between occupational segregation and wage discrimination.[58] If women are segregated or, as our critic prefers, concentrated into certain jobs, the women will be paid less than the men.

Another source of evidence that women are underpaid is composed of cases in which employers purport to use objective criteria to set compensation and pay men's jobs what the criteria indicate, but pay women's jobs less than the criteria indicate. A good example of this form of sex discrimination is the case of *General Electric and Westinghouse,* decided by the War Labor Board in 1945.[59] In essence, the union convinced the board that women's jobs were undervalued and underpaid. Another example is the recent case of *County of Washington* v. *Gunther,* in which jail matrons were prepared to prove that, although the county had evaluated their jobs and the evaluation showed they should be paid 95 percent as much as the male guards, the county actually paid the matrons only 70 percent as much as the guards.[60] Similar evidence is provided by a study commissioned by the State of Washington that revealed in 1974 that state jobs held mainly by women were paid only 80 percent of what comparably valued jobs held mainly by men were paid.[61]

CRITIC   Again I must caution against building an argument on two cases, especially when one was decided in the 1940s and the other in the 1980s.

ADVOCATE   Which goes to prove nothing has changed in forty years! But I do not rest my argument on court cases alone. Social scientists have developed systematic methods for determining whether women's work is underpaid throughout the economy. In one study, the question asked was whether the skill difference in men's and women's work could explain the lower pay the women received. The Department of Labor publishes the *Dictionary of Occupational Titles* that scores four thousand jobs according to the skills they require. The scholars divided the skills measured in the dictionary into five categories: training, cognitive skills, visual perception skills, manual skills, and social skills. It was found that women's jobs required the same schooling as men's jobs, though the latter required, and provided, more on-the-job training. Cognitive skills required of men's and women's jobs were equal. Visual perception skills were also equal, though somewhat different: men's jobs required more space and form perception, while women's jobs required more clerical perception (that is, seeing detail in written or tabular material). Men's and women's jobs were equal on some aspects of manual skill, namely, dexterity and eye-hand-foot coordination; but men's jobs required slightly more motor coordination, substantially more strength, and entailed greater complexity in dealing with physical objects. Women's jobs required more social skills, but analysis revealed an important distinction between power and nurturing. The social skills needed for women's jobs involved more nurturing, for example, teaching and counseling; the social skills needed for men's jobs involved more power, for example, persuading and managing. This much of the study demolished the common assumption that men's jobs require more skill than women's jobs.

The next step in the study was to relate differences in skills to compensation. By calculating how much the earnings gap would decrease if men and women had the same mean on each job characteristic, the researchers were able to estimate how much of the gap was caused by skill and how much by sex. For example, about 10 percent of the gap was attributed to men's greater on-the-job training, and another 8 percent was explained by men's concentration in jobs requiring social skills involving power instead of nurturing. Skills in which men and women were equal, of course, explained none of the gap. And one skill in which men exceeded women actually decreased the gap: men had more manual skills than women, but manual skills had a negative rate of return for workers, so women's lower use of such skills enhanced rather than diminished female compensation. After controlling for the type and level of skills that various occupations demand, the scholars concluded that the average sex composition of occupations explained one-third of the wage gap. In other words, when skills are equalized, one-third of the difference between the average men's and women's pay results from underpayment of women who hold predominantly female jobs. The compensation of men who work in such jobs also suffers.[62]

CRITIC   I have two points to make about this study. First, there are few if any other studies like it. Social science methodology is not developed enough to place much trust in the results of one or two or even three pieces of such research. Second, these studies are far from conclusive. I happen to be familiar with the study our advocate discussed, and I know that one of the authors of the study has acknowledged that alternative explanations of the results are possible.[63] For example, blue-collar men are concentrated in durable goods manufacturing industries that are capital intensive, oligopolistic, and unionized, and these three characteristics may allow the employers to pay higher wages than employers in industries in which women typically work. Also, crowding of women into a narrow range of occupations might drive down the price of women's work. To the extent that either of these explanations is valid, women are not underpaid for their work, but merely hold jobs that do not pay well. Those jobs would not pay any better if they were held by men. Here I will repeat the point I made before: the right solution is to enforce existing law so as to open all job opportunities to all qualified workers, not to raise the pay of workers who occupy jobs that deserve low pay.

ADVOCATE   Without conceding any weakness in the methodology or the conclusions of the study I have just discussed—indeed, our critic has all but admitted the existence of the dual labor market—I will discuss another sort of study. The one I have just described tried to account for the earnings gap in terms of the characteristics of jobs. Another type of study tries to account for the gap in terms of the characteristics of workers.[64] The idea underlying these human capital studies is the neoclassical economic belief that the wage rate of a job equals the marginal productivity of the last worker hired: workers are paid exactly the value of their economic contribution to a firm. If a worker's economic contribution, or productivity, could be measured, the existence of wage discrimination could be confirmed or denied by comparing the wages of equally productive male and female workers. Unfortunately, productivity generally cannot be measured. Except for certain jobs, commonly involving the production of physical goods and paid by piece rate, such as sewing buttons on shirts, productivity remains an abstraction.

Nevertheless, indirect measures of productivity have been found. On the theory that compensation within a homogeneous class of workers, in which discrimination is not an issue, tends to reflect productivity, workers' characteristics associated with rates of compensation have been identified, for example, education, on-the-job training, experience, and continuity of work history. If productivity is in fact associated with these characteristics, which can be measured directly, the characteristics may serve as proxies for productivity and permit comparisons across classes. That is, if education, experience, and so forth are associated with white males' compensation, it is reasonable to suppose the same characteristics are associated with females' compensation as well, and thus it is possible to use these characteristics as proxies in productivity comparisons between white males and females.

Using data from national samples of the working population, several scholars have applied the human capital approach and found a substantial unexplained earnings gap between men and women.[65] In these studies, the difference between men's and women's productivity—that is, the differences in men's and women's possession of the characteristics believed to be proxies for productivity—accounted for only a small portion of the earnings gap between the sexes. In most of the studies, less than 20 percent of the gap could be attributed to worker characteristics; in none of the studies was more than half the gap explained.[66] The portion of the wage gap that cannot be explained by worker characteristics is called the residual, and it is believed that an unmeasured female characteristic must account for the residual. Because most or all legitimate characteristics that explain white males' productivity have been measured, the likely candidate for the unmeasured characteristic causing the earnings gap is sex discrimination.

CRITIC   I believe there are serious problems with the human capital studies to which you have alluded. Before I expose those problems, however, I really must point out that you have contradicted yourself. You have relied on studies whose assumptions are inconsistent with other studies you have also relied on. Human capital research makes the traditional neoclassical assumptions about labor markets, namely, that employers compete for workers and workers compete for jobs. These competitions create supply and demand curves. By comparing the productivity and compensation of men and women, the human capitalists assume that men and women are functioning in a unitary labor market. But you have already relied on the theory of a segmented labor market to prove that men and women function in a dual market. Across the dual market, it would not be surprising that persons with equal human capital receive disparate compensation.[67] So I think you have to make a choice of labor market models and stick to it.

Turning now to the human capital studies, a number of economists reject the marginal productivity theory of wages on which the studies rely. It is plausible that custom, union strength, and the economic position of a firm or industry can affect wages. Another problem with human capital studies is that wages may not reflect the entire compensation of a job. People often trade some take-home pay for a desirable community, a pleasant working environment, job security, opportunity for promotion, and the like. Willingness to make such trade-offs may well vary across classes of people. Personally, I am convinced that women prefer clean, indoor, hazard-free jobs and will sacrifice pay for them. Suppose, for example, a woman has a choice between job

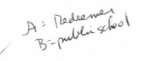

A = Redeemer
B - public school

A, which is personally satisfying but pays only x dollars, and job B, which is unpleasant but pays $x + y$ dollars. If her husband has a good job, she might be more willing to accept job A. I suspect more women than men find themselves in this fortunate position.

Even accepting the premises on which the human capital studies are based, significant problems remain. One obvious problem is the risk of omitting a relevant variable. Certainly it is difficult to assert with confidence that every characteristic affecting compensation has been captured by any given model. If a relevant and legitimate characteristic were omitted, the residual would be larger than it should be, and the earnings gap (or part of it) would be blamed on discrimination when the gap (or part of it) should have been attributed to a legitimate cause.

Another problem with the human capital studies is that the proxies for productivity may be false. An example is experience. Experience may reflect job-related learning that occurs at work. If so, greater experience is probably a good indicator of greater productivity. But while most people learn something when they begin to work, many do not continue to learn on the job, and experience often reflects mere seniority. It is well known that seniority can be related to higher wages without being related to higher productivity.

Yet another problem with human capital studies concerns the meaning of scores on proxies. Numbers that are the same on paper may represent very different degrees of productivity. For example, two persons may each have completed sixteen years of school, but one studied ancient Scandinavian runes in college while the other studied business and accounting. Results based on the assumption that these two persons received educations of equal quality and relevance to their jobs can be misleading. I cannot say with certainty that this problem systematically biases the male-

female comparisons in human capital studies, though I suspect it does. For example, women's tendency toward liberal
arts curricula may lessen the relevance of women's college
degrees to job performance. But I can say with certainty
that the problem of misleading scores on proxies diminishes
my faith in the outcomes of human capital research.

I will mention one last problem with the human capital
studies. Unexplained residuals are just that—unexplained—
and nothing more. It is possible that illegitimate factors that
correlate with sex may account for the residuals, but it seems
as possible that legitimate factors that correlate with sex
may also account for the residuals.[68]

ADVOCATE   No study is perfect. There is always more
to learn. But this does not mean we should ignore what
we have already learned. The scholars who use the human
capital approach are fully aware of the problems you have
mentioned, and they employ many sophisticated techniques
to minimize these problems. I think the results are trust-
worthy and are a sufficient basis for action—at least until
someone comes up with better techniques that yield different
conclusions.

As for my contradicting myself, I need say only that I
will fight you on any ground you choose. I think the competitive model of the labor market is false for most women—
and many men as well, for example, blacks and other minorities. But if you persist in resorting to the competitive
model, I will cite the human capital studies to defeat you
on your own assumptions.

Now let us get on with the issues. Other proof that
women are underpaid comes from a comparison of women
who never marry and men. An unmarried woman generally
enters the job market at a young age and works without
interruption throughout her life. She does not typically rear

children or allow household duties to interfere with her career. She is willing to commute from home to office, to work as many hours as a man, and to invest in herself through on-the-job training. And she is free to climb the promotion ladder by moving from city to city. Nevertheless, the average income of women age twenty-five to sixty-four who have never married is only 65 percent of the average income of men of the same age.[69] Surely this fact alone is evidence that women are underpaid and that a great deal of the earnings gap must be attributed to sex discrimination.

CRITIC   I think not, for two reasons. First, the comparison is misleading because these two classes are different from one another in an important way: average age and, therefore, experience and seniority. The class of never-married working women is much younger than the class of all working men.[70] The reason is obvious. When a working woman marries, she may continue to work, but she leaves the class of never-married women. Therefore, for purposes of this comparison, she ceases to accumulate experience and seniority. But when a working man marries, he remains in the class of all working men, and he goes right on accumulating experience and seniority. So the average working man has more experience and seniority than the average never-married working woman, and it is no surprise that his earnings are higher.

My second reason is that a much more informative comparison is between never-married working men and never-married working women. On the assumptions that most members of both of these classes begin to work upon completing their educations and continue to work throughout their lives, the average age, and hence experience and seniority, of the two classes ought to be similar. The Bureau of Labor Statistics has made such a comparison and reports that in 1979 the median usual weekly earnings of never-married women were 84 percent of the earnings of never-married men.[71] A gap still appears, but there is a big difference between a gap of 35 percent and a gap of 16 percent. And I think a sizeable portion of the 16 percent gap can be explained. A never-married working woman age forty-five may, at the age of fifteen or thirty, have expected to marry and rear a family. At fifteen she may have chosen homemaking courses in high school; at thirty she may have decided against switching to a job with enhanced opportunity for promotion but less immediate income. Thus, her desire to marry and rear a family may have led her to invest less in her human capital than a man would have invested.[72]

A<small>DVOCATE</small>   Sixteen percent—$3,200 out of a salary of $20,000, which amounts to $160,000 (without interest or inflation) over a fifty-year career—is nothing to sneeze at. I am surprised you admit to so much injustice against women.

The last sort of evidence I will cite to prove how and why women are underpaid comes from examination of the process of collective bargaining. Until 1965, unions had no duty under federal law to admit women to membership, although a union that excluded women could nevertheless represent them for purposes of collective bargaining. Why would women choose to be represented by a union that would not admit them to membership? Most likely, the women were part of a bargaining unit composed mostly of men, and the majority of the unit favored the union. Although such a union had a legal duty to represent the women fairly, the women could not participate in the deliberations leading to the union's demand on the employer. Women could not sit on the negotiating committee, could not vote on ratification of the contract, and could not run for union office or vote in union elections to oust an officer who ignored their interests. It is no wonder that unions did little to end occupational segregation or to increase the pay for women's work.

Since 1965, federal law has required unions to admit women to membership. Nevertheless, if a majority of a bargaining unit is male, important issues may be decided against women. For example, suppose the question is whether to ask for a 7 percent raise for all jobs or for a 75-cent raise for all jobs. Either choice seems equitable, but if women are concentrated in the lower paying jobs, the choice will have an important effect on women's interests. Increasingly, unions are responding to women's voices. Some women have reached high positions in unions. Women have organized into groups to advance their interests through the labor movement, and, perhaps most important, women are participating in local union affairs. But this is a recent phenomenon. Until the past decade, most unions were content to go along with their employers' discriminatory pay practices.[73]

CRITIC   If collective bargaining shows signs of narrowing the earnings gap, this is so much more a reason to keep the heavy hand of the government out of private matters.

MODERATOR   I believe we have covered the earnings gap in sufficient detail. Let us turn now to the role job evaluation plays—

ADVOCATE   If I may, I want to interrupt to mention just one last fact that is not directly relevant to the earnings gap in America, but nonetheless puts the gap into context.

In some societies, anthropologists tell us, men fish and women weave, and fishing is considered more important than weaving. In other societies, men weave and women fish, and weaving is considered more important than fishing.[74] The conclusion is obvious. Women's work is under-valued everywhere, and American is no exception.

MODERATOR   That said, let us move on—

CRITIC   I'm sorry, but I feel I must say that, for once, I agree with our advocate on something. I agree that the evidence about men's fishing and women's weaving, or the other way around, proves very little. In fact, in modern societies, in which there is general agreement as to the relative prestige of jobs, what may be a man's job in one society may be a woman's job in another.[75]

In sum, the evidence presented by our advocate that women are paid less for their work than men would be paid is inconclusive, ambiguous, and perhaps self-contradictory. As a result, this drive for comparable worth—whatever it means—lacks a basis in fact.

MODERATOR   And now we will turn to the role job evaluation plays in the debate over comparable worth.

ADVOCATE   While I of course regard more highly the evidence I have offered that women are underpaid, I would like to meet the challenge implied in our critic's last comment and make clear exactly what comparable worth means and that it has a very firm basis in fact.

Comparable worth is the idea that an employer should

pay men and women equally for jobs that are equally valuable to a firm. This idea can be implemented through job evaluation, which is a way of measuring the value of a job. If two jobs are assigned the same value, employees holding those jobs are entitled to receive the same compensation—seniority and other legitimate factors being equal—regardless of what the compensation for those jobs may be in the labor market. In fact, because the labor market discriminates so markedly against women's jobs, as I think I have already proved, the less attention an employer pays to the market, the fairer that employer's compensation system is likely to be.

Really, there is no single accepted form of job evaluation. There are many ways a firm can set the compensation of its employees, and there are many forms of job evaluation plans in use. The one I consider the most fully developed and the most easily adapted to bias-free implementation is called the factor point method. It begins by identifying a set of compensable factors, which are elements considered to be legitimate bases for pay differentials among jobs. Then scales are devised for measuring the extent to which the various factors are associated with jobs. Next, to take into account that some factors are more important than others, the factors are weighted. Finally, each job is scored on the various scales; the weightings are applied; and each job receives a total score. For example, a common compensable factor is working conditions. Suppose jobs in a firm in northern Michigan are performed under one of three distinct working conditions: a comfortable office, a noisy assembly line, and an outdoor yard. The scale for working conditions might range from 1 to 3, yet the weight assigned to the score might be heavy. Thus, for the purpose of calculating a job's total points, the score on working conditions might be multiplied by a factor of 50. Another common compensable factor is responsibility for others' work. Suppose some employees in the firm work alone, while others supervise many persons. The scale for responsibility might range from 1 to 25. Yet the firm might believe that responsibility of this sort is of relatively minor importance to overall operations and assign a relatively light weight to this factor. Thus, for the purpose of calculating a job's total points, the score on responsibility for others' work might be multiplied by a factor of 10.

How compensable factors are chosen and weighted is very important. One method selects factors and weights them so as to replicate the firm's existing pay structure. This method is called policy-capturing because it makes explicit the unarticulated system actually in use. I have already expressed my opinion about how most employers treat women's jobs, so I need not comment extensively on the policy-capturing method of selecting and weighting compensable factors. Suffice it to say that this method tends to etch on stone the inequities that already exist.

The other principal method of selecting and weighting compensable factors is based on beliefs as to the legitimate bases of compensation. This method is called a priori because the factors and their weights are determined before jobs are scored. In an organized setting, the union and the employer would probably negotiate over the compensable factors and their weights; in a nonunion setting, the employer would probably decide these unilaterally, using information and advice supplied by a consultant. With the policy-capturing method, one knows in advance that the highest paid job will receive the highest score, the lowest paid job will receive the lowest score, and jobs in between will follow suit. With the a priori method, one knows nothing in advance. A low-paying job might get a fairly high score, and that would be a signal the job was underpaid. For example, many people think nurses are underpaid by hospitals and that a priori job evaluation would correct this situation. Of course, a high-paying job might get a low score, and that would be a signal the job was overpaid. For example, brick layers are often paid more than carpenters. Perhaps in the past, when bricks were laid by stone masons, who were more skilled than carpenters, this relationship was appropriate. But today carpenters are often more skilled than brick layers, and a priori job evaluation could lift the heavy hand of history from the wage structure.[76]

Now I do not want to convey the impression that I think job evaluation, particularly as it is practiced today, is perfect. It is not perfect. It has serious practical problems. I have already mentioned how the policy-capturing method carries discrimination from the labor market into the firm, and I want to discuss a few other problems. Nevertheless, I believe that the problems can be overcome and that job evaluation is women's best bet for attaining equal compensation for their labor.

One problem is—

CRITIC   I think job evaluation can serve valuable purposes if handled properly, though I agree it has some practical problems. But I would like to interpose a theoretical objection before we proceed any further. I consider it a fundamental point, or I would not interrupt our advocate to raise it.

The objection is that comparable worth focuses on the demand side of the labor market, to the exclusion of the supply side, and misuses job evaluation for this reason. Let me elaborate on an excellent example given by Sharon Smith. Suppose an employer in the business of providing simultaneous translations for speakers had offices in Miami and Montreal. If the employer needed to fill two jobs in Miami, one requiring translation from Spanish to English and the other requiring translation from French to English, surely a qualified Spanish–English translator could be hired at a lower wage than a qualified French–English translator. But if the employer needed to fill two such jobs in Montreal, the wage rates would probably be reversed. Most people see nothing wrong with this situation; it simply reflects the law of supply and demand. Would our reaction change if we learned the employer had a job evaluation plan that rated the two jobs equally?

Consider this modification of the foregoing example. Suppose the employer needed not only Spanish–English and French–English translators in Miami, but also Russian–English, German–English, and Loma–English translators. All these jobs rated equally on the employer's job evaluation plan. Suppose further that most of the qualified Spanish–English translators in Miami were women, while most of the other translators were men. In other words, suppose Spanish–English translating were women's work in Miami, while French-, Russian-, and Loma–English translating were men's work in Miami. Is this case any different from the foregoing one?

There simply is no inherent value to a job, just as there is no inherent value to an ounce of gold or an acre of real estate. A thing is worth what people are willing to pay for it, and labor is no different. Compensation is a function of the supply of and the demand for labor.

Let me hasten to repeat that I do not object to job evaluation. It can be useful so long as it remains tied to the labor market. For example, if a firm has some jobs that are unique—that is, jobs that have no easily known price in the labor market—job evaluation can be used to set equitable compensation for these unique jobs vis-à-vis other jobs that do have a price in the market. But it is essential that the job evaluation plan be firmly anchored to the labor market.

I expect I will make this final point again, but I think it is appropriate to say now that to the extent comparable worth ignores supply and demand, the whole idea will prove impracticable and counterproductive.

ADVOCATE   I think your point is indeed fundamental, as is your error.

You assume the labor market operates the same way for women as for men. In fact, it does not. Men are not socialized into preparing for low-paying work before they enter the labor market; men are not excluded from high-paying work once they are in the market; and men are not crowded into a small number of occupations. The value of labor may be its price in a free market, but women are not part of a free market. For women, the labor market is segmented, and they are relegated to the secondary segment. For every case like the female Spanish-English translators in Miami, there are dozens of cases of women who are hired into low-paying, dead-end jobs while equally qualified men are hired into high-paying jobs with unlimited opportunities for advancement. How many men have been excluded from apprenticeship and on-the-job training programs because of sex? How many men have been refused consideration for promotion to supervisory or managerial positions because of sex? How many men with years of experience have trained a newly hired woman and six months later seen that woman preferred for promotion?

Women may participate in a competitive labor market, but their competitors are other women and the jobs for which women compete are artificially limited. The price of women's labor is not the result of supply and demand but of bloated supply and strangled demand. Job evaluation is simply a tool to reform an unfair, noncompetitive market and to put women in the same position as men in a free market.

And now I will return to the points I wanted to make about the practical problems of job evaluation—

CRITIC   Please do. I am the last to interfere with such a worthwhile effort.

ADVOCATE   —and how they can be overcome. I will mention five problems. The first is the source of job descriptions and their accuracy. Someone observing—even supervising—a job may not fully appreciate its duties and responsibilities. An inaccurate or incomplete job description will lead to a wrongly valued job every time.[77]

The second problem concerns compensable factors, and it has three aspects. One aspect is that, if the factors are not well fitted to the jobs to which the factors are applied, the scores on the jobs will be misleading. For example, one choosing the compensable factors for the job of hod carrier would likely include physical effort but exclude ability to function well under time pressure. If the hod carrier's job evaluation plan were applied to a word processor in an executive office, the latter job would be wrongly underrated. Another aspect of the problem with compensable factors is how they are implemented. For example, suppose effort is chosen as a compensable factor. Effort can be measured by the amount of necessary strength or by the degree of resulting fatigue. The hod carrier may score high on either dimension, but the word processor would score high only on the latter. Therefore, using strength instead of fatigue will underrate the word processor's job. A third aspect of the problem with compensable factors is the weight assigned to them.[78] (Variability of scores can also be important in this connection, but for simplicity I will assume that jobs are scored evenly over the full range of possible scores.) Suppose both physical effort and ability to perform under pressure are compensable factors, and each is rated on a scale of 1 to 10. But suppose also that physical effort is weighted three times more heavily than ability to perform under pres-

sure. The word processor might get a 1 for physical effort (which would be multiplied by 3 to reflect its weighting) and a 10 for ability to perform under pressure (which would be multiplied by 1) for a combined score of 13. The hod carrier might get a 10 for physical effort (which would be multiplied by 3) and a 1 for ability to perform under pressure (which would be multiplied by 1) for a combined score of 31. Of course, these two ratings would be added together with weighted ratings on other compensable factors to produce a total score, but the hod carrier's extra 18 points—derived from the improper weighting of physical effort vis- ?
à-vis ability to function under pressure—will contribute to the earnings gap.

A third problem with job evaluation is that it requires judgment, and judgment can be biased. Judgment is in-volved in describing the tasks and responsibilities of jobs and in rating a job against the compensable factors. I regret that at the present time, there is considerable evidence that sex bias infects judgments about the worth of women's jobs. Some of the evidence is experimental, and some of it is empirical.

The experimental evidence shows that female workers are less highly regarded than male workers with identical characteristics.[79] This evidence comes from experimental studies in social psychology in which subjects are presented with a set of vignettes that describe the performance or qualifications of individuals and then are asked to rate the individuals in some way. The sex of the individuals is varied to determine whether it influenced the ratings. Invariably, women are rated below men. For example, chairmen of psychology departments in colleges were sent descriptions of psychologists and asked to indicate for each one whether he or she might be hired and, if so, at what level. The names attached to the descriptions were systematically al-tered from male to female in order to determine whether the sex of the "candidates" affected their desirability. It was found that male names were on average 10 percent more likely to be judged worthy of appointment at the tenured level than female names with otherwise identical descriptions.[80] In another study using similar methodology, bank managers at a management institute regarded employees with male names as more suitable for promotion, more likely to be chosen to attend a professional training conference, and more likely to have their recommendations accepted regarding resolution of a conflict between a supervisor and a subordinate. Because job evaluators commonly know the sex of the workers performing a job, there is a great risk that women's jobs are underrated simply because of the sex of the incumbents.[81]

The empirical evidence comes from studies of existing compensation plans. In the leading study, an independent firm was commissioned by the State of Washington in 1974 to examine pay differences between predominately male and female job classes and to evaluate those differences against an objective measure of job worth. It was impossible to study all forty-five hundred state job classifications, so a sample of 121 classifications representing approximately 13,600 employees was chosen. Fifty-nine of these classifications were dominated by men (that is, 70 percent or more of the employees were men), and 62 were dominated by women. Job content was determined from the state's job descriptions, questionnaires, and interviews, and the jobs were point-rated according to knowledge and skill, mental demands, accountability, and working conditions. The results were as predictable as they were outrageous: female jobs were paid less than male jobs receiving the same or fewer points; the pay differentials ranged from 22 percent to 35 percent.

A follow-up study was performed by the same firm in 1976 for the purpose of developing a fair salary structure based on the 1974 data. The salary each classification would receive in the absence of discrimination was estimated. Here are two revealing examples. First, Park Ranger (male) received 181 points and was paid at salary level 24. Homemaker I (female) received 182 points and was paid at salary level 19. Park Ranger and Homemaker were thus virtually identical in worth, yet the men were paid five levels higher than the women. In the absence of discrimination, the women would have been paid at the same level as the men. Second, Chemist II (male) received 277 points and was paid at level 33. Registered Nurse IV (female) received 573 points and was paid at level 31. The women's job was worth more than twice as much as the men's job, yet the women were paid less than the men. In the absence of discrimination, the nurses would have been paid at level 39, six levels above the chemists.

An independent firm also studied jobs offered by the State of Connecticut. The study found in 1979 that predominantly male jobs were paid from 8 percent to 18 percent more than predominantly female jobs rated at comparable levels of worth. Mixed jobs (less than 70 percent of either sex) were paid at a mean rate.[82]

CRITIC   If sex bias were truly shown to influence job ratings, I would agree wholeheartedly on the need to eliminate the bias. But the empirical studies our advocate has just summarized do not prove anything about sex bias. All the studies prove is that different people have different opinions about the value of a job. Someone thought registered nurses were worth 573 points. Someone else thought chemists were worth more. We have no reason to believe these differences were not maintained in good faith.

In fact, we have reason to believe the differences were genuine. There is solid evidence that, when women perform job evaluation, they rate jobs at the same levels men do.[83]

ADVOCATE   Which proves the problem is in the system, not in the people. But the problem is just as real.

CRITIC   No, I think the problem is that jobs just don't have any intrinsic worth, and various attempts to manufacture worth will be inconsistent with each other because the initial assumptions about what is valuable will differ.

ADVOCATE   A job may have no intrinsic worth, but it may have relative worth—that is, a value as compared to another job. And judgments about the relative value of jobs can certainly be colored by sex bias. Let me give one specific example of how discrimination in judgment can occur. In *Thompson* v. *Boyle,* female bindery workers sued the Government Printing Office, claiming their work was equal to that of male bookbinders. The government's job evaluator, Dr. L——, assigned 48 points to male jobs for lifting certain weights and assigned 12 points to female jobs for lifting the same weights. Dr. L—— awarded points to men for handling confidential data and awarded no points to women who handled the same material. The court also found that Dr. L—— underestimated the experience and skill factors in the women's work and ignored the training required for their jobs. Finally, and most revealing, Dr. L—— testified that he awarded women no points for training or experience in hand sewing "because the sewing was of the variety most women knew how to perform."[84] Isn't that incredible! I wonder whether this walking atavism refused to award points to men for following written instructions because men knew how to read before they started working!
    I would like to point out two further problems with job evaluation. One is that many firms utilize two or more discrete evaluation plans.[85] For example, there may be a plan

for shop jobs, another for office jobs, and a third for executive jobs. When more than one plan is used, comparing jobs rated by different plans is certainly difficult and perhaps impractical. The alternative is a single plan for all jobs in a firm, but this alternative requires solution of all three aspects of the first problem I mentioned concerning compensable factors.

A final problem with job evaluation applies chiefly to the policy-capturing method. The mathematics of creating appropriate models are highly sophisticated. Some social scientists charge that the techniques used in creating these models have not kept pace with developments in econometrics, psychometrics, and sociological measurement.[86] To the extent this charge is valid, job evaluation plans may be unreliable indices of job worth.

CRITIC   If job evaluation were a human being, I would not want to be his life insurance company! With all these problems, what earthly use is it to comparable worth?

ADVOCATE   The problems are significant, but they have solutions. I favor the factor point method because antibias safeguards can be built into it. It should be substituted for other methods as widely as possible. I believe jobs can be accurately described, especially if we involve employees in the process. I believe compensable factors can be fitted to jobs and implemented in appropriate ways by validating the factors in the same way we validate selection criteria to avoid discrimination in hiring and promoting. We can weight compensable factors fairly by using regression analysis that predicts the pay of white males, who are not victims of discrimination in the labor market, and applying the resulting equations to jobs held by women. I think there is no escaping the need for a single plan for an entire firm, but I am sure a plan fair to all jobs can be developed if we implement the suggestions I have just mentioned. We can avoid bias in judgment by utilizing several persons of both sexes to describe jobs and rate jobs against compensable factors. There are mathematicians with skills equal to the tasks I have outlined. We need only call upon them.

CRITIC   Notice our advocate believes this can be done, and thinks that can be done, and has no doubts something else can be done, but does not say these things *have* been done. They have not in fact been done. Job evaluation is an imperfect instrument. It is useful for some purposes, but I have serious reservations about using it to revolutionize compensation practices.

More important, there is another feature of job evaluation that our advocate has conveniently ignored, namely, the way compensation is assigned to jobs. However compensable factors are chosen and implemented and weighted, and however jobs are rated against the compensable factors, the end result is simply a hierarchy of jobs—an ordinal but not a cardinal ranking. Job evaluation does not establish the level of compensation for each job. Of course, the theory is that higher rated jobs ought to be paid more than lower rated jobs, but the theory can be satisfied in many ways. I suppose the purist would insist that a dollar value should be assigned to each point a job receives. For example, if the lowest job received 40 points and each point were worth 10 cents an hour, the pay for that job would be $4.00 an hour. And if the highest job received 400 points, the pay would be $40.00 an hour. But I doubt that such a straight-line approach is used widely—in fact, I doubt it is used at all—since real problems would quickly develop because of the labor market. Even our advocate admits the labor market exists and assigns prices to jobs. Suppose in my example the job rated at 50 points and paid $5.00 an hour was lathe operator and suppose the going wage for lathe operators was $5.75. The firm could not attract lathe operators, and it would lose any it trained. What I am trying to point out is that a firm just cannot ignore the labor market.

In fact, job evaluation as it is commonly practiced takes express account of the labor market. Typically, after all the jobs have been scored, the job evaluators identify those jobs in the firm that have analogues in the labor market. These are called "key jobs" or "bench marks" and, because a number of employers offer the same job, there are prices for such jobs in the market. These prices are adopted as the compensation for the key jobs.[87] Jobs with scores between the ratings for key jobs have no market analogues, so some kind of interpolation is necessary. This is where mathematics comes in. Frankly, however, I am not concerned about interpolations. My point is that job evaluation as used today is sensitive to prices in the labor market.

I appreciate our advocate's argument here. Policy-capturing job evaluation plans are objectionable because they perpetuate discrimination against women. And I must agree that, if the labor market does discriminate against women, job evaluation will bring that discrimination into the firm. But I cannot imagine how, in a free market economy, a firm could ignore the market and survive.

ADVOCATE   I need to clarify my position. I oppose policy-capturing job evaluation because it is designed to reproduce, in fancy equations, an employer's existing pay practices. It cannot correct inequities against women's jobs because its express purpose is to rationalize an existing structure in which women's jobs are undervalued. Therefore, I support a priori job evaluation, which can reform pay practices. I am convinced that if a priori job evaluation is done fairly, women's work will be rated substantially higher than it is now and women's earnings will rise commensurately.

I think it is clear that existing compensation practices are biased against women's work, and this statement includes assigning compensation to jobs. If there is bias in the labor market against women's work, the bench mark method of setting pay will import that bias into the firm. Indeed, the process is commonly aggravated by comparing men's jobs in the firm to men's jobs in the community, and likewise for women's jobs.[88] Another vicious circle develops. After surveying the labor market, a given employer sets pay. Then these pay rates become part of the labor market to which other employers refer. But if bias is eliminated from job evaluation and from the labor market, women's jobs will be interspersed with men's jobs throughout the hierarchies within the firm and without. Then if jobs in the firm are compared with jobs in the community, each job will be paid according to its worth, and that rate will be the same as its market price. Once bias is eliminated from the system, I have no objection to an employer's referring to the labor market to find the price of a job. But until bias is eliminated, women's jobs will continue to be undervalued, and comparable worth is the remedy for that kind of discrimination.

MODERATOR   Perhaps this is an appropriate moment for us to turn to the consequences of comparable worth. What effects can be foreseen if comparable worth is adopted?

ADVOCATE   Women will be paid what their work is worth!

CRITIC   Our advocate makes comparable worth sound so simple and so right. Yet I think a moment's reflection will reveal that the push for comparable worth is nothing more than a maneuver by an interest group that is trying to better its position in our society at the expense of other groups. The basic fact to keep in mind is that comparable worth makes only one change: the price of women's labor to employers increases. Productivity does not increase. Therefore, because the total amount of goods and services remains constant while women doing women's work receive a larger share of the total, other groups must receive less.

Who will gain and who will lose? The only gainers will be women who hold women's jobs. Who the losers will be depends on how employers respond to their higher payroll costs. If the employers raise prices, the losers will be the victims of the resulting inflation. This group includes retirees, welfare recipients, disabled workers, and employed persons and their families who lack the economic power to keep pace with inflation. In the alternative, employers may reduce, or slow the rate of growth of, other workers' earnings. In this case, the losers would be men, women doing nontraditional—that is, men's—work, and the families dependent on these workers' earnings. A third possibility is that employers will substitute capital for labor, in which event the principal losers would be some of the very women who expected to gain so much. Nine secretaries working at word processors might become more cost-effective than twelve secretaries working at typewriters. Because each employer will respond according to the particular situation, all three of these possibilities will probably occur to one degree or another. Therefore, comparable worth will increase inflationary pressures, decrease the compensation for men's jobs, and disemploy women.[89]

If that is not enough, comparable worth may well be

counterproductive for women in the long run. If we accept our advocate's argument that occupational concentration causes underpayment of women's work, comparable worth will widen the earnings gap by exacerbating occupational concentration: for if the pay of women's work is increased, the incentive for women to take other kinds of jobs will be proportionately diminished. The more a woman can earn as a secretary or an elementary school teacher, the less will be her desire to train for, and overcome the barriers to, jobs now reserved for men.

ADVOCATE   That is a long bill of particulars, but I will respond to each charge. Let me begin by pointing out that you contradicted yourself when you predicted that comparable worth will increase female unemployment and exacerbate occupational segregation. If some women do lose their jobs, this will have two consequences. First, disemployed women will be strongly motivated to crash the barriers to men's jobs. Second, girls who are preparing for careers will perceive there are fewer traditional women's jobs available—no matter how well such jobs pay—and the girls will have good reason to prepare for nontraditional jobs. So I doubt we will see both increased female unemployment and increased occupational segregation.

Next, I reject the argument that comparable worth will be counterproductive because it will exacerbate occupational segregation. For three reasons, two economic and one non-economic, I think just the opposite will occur. My first economic reason is that, if the pay of women's jobs goes up, some men will be attracted to those jobs, and that will simultaneously open some formerly men's jobs to women. My second economic reason follows from my agreement with our critic that comparable worth may lead to some increase in female unemployment. As I have already mentioned, disemployed women will cross the barricades into men's jobs, and girls, realizing there are fewer women's jobs, will thus prepare themselves for men's jobs. My non-economic reason is a terribly powerful phenomenon in modern America: the women's liberation movement. Today's women will not allow themselves to be segregated into menial jobs. Doubling or quadrupling the pay of a secretary will not keep her daughter from going to law school—and may even make it possible. So comparable worth will not worsen occupational segregation.

Finally, I readily agree that comparable worth is part of the effort to better women's position in society. In this sense, the effort is no different from the abolition movement in the nineteenth century, which sought to better blacks' position in society. The important question is the justice of the effort. Women ask only to be paid what they contribute to a firm. To the extent women are paid less than they are worth, who can deny they are being exploited? Of course, ending this exploitation cannot be painless, and those who now benefit the most from it are likely to cry the loudest about its end. But justice demands an end to it. If righting a wrong has some undesirable side effects, the answer is not to ignore the wrong but to remedy the side effects equitably. So if comparable worth would contribute slightly to inflation, that would be no excuse to condone the underpayment of women's work. Rather, the effects of inflation should be mitigated by programs that spread the cost of mitigation broadly throughout society. Failing to remedy women's undercompensation for fear of the impact on society's defenseless classes allocates to women a disproportionate share of the burden of caring for these unfortunate people.

If comparable worth will decrease the compensation for men's jobs, the reason is that men are now being overpaid with money that is generated by women's labor. I can see nothing wrong with putting an end to this unjust enrichment and paying each worker according to his or her productivity. And if comparable worth will disemploy some women because employers substitute capital for labor, the substitution should be encouraged. Human and physical resources are inefficiently allocated when the price of labor is kept artificially below its true value.

CRITIC   I am pleased to hear you begin to discuss efficiency and allocation of resources because you have revealed a basic error in your thinking. You have said more than once that a woman should be paid according to her true worth to a firm. True worth in this lexicon is a synonym for economic contribution or marginal productivity. Your error is in confusing the metaphysical concept of inherent worth with the economic concept of market value. If this distinction is ignored and comparable worth is adopted, I am convinced the mechanism for allocating resources in our economy will be seriously damaged, if not altogether destroyed, and the result will be enormous inefficiencies or outright government control of labor.

I have mentioned before that there is no inherent value to a job, just as there is no inherent value to an ounce of gold. I don't have scripture to support my point, but I can quote what Adam Smith knew two hundred years ago (and our advocate has apparently forgotten).

The word VALUE, it is to be observed, has two different meanings, and sometimes expresses the utility of some particular object, and sometimes the power of purchasing other goods which the possession of that object conveys. The one may be called "value in use;" the other, "value in exchange." The things which have the greatest value in use have frequently little or no value in exchange; and on the contrary, those which have the greatest value in exchange have frequently little or no value in use. Nothing is more useful than water: but it will purchase scarce any thing;

scarce any thing can be had in exchange for it. A diamond, on the contrary, has scarce any value in use; but a very great quantity of other goods may frequently be had in exchange for it.[90]

Water is more valuable than diamonds because we cannot live without water, but diamonds cost more than water. Yet the paradox is only apparent. As Adam Smith said, the word *value* has two different meanings. Our advocate uses the word in its sense of value in use and equates a score on a job evaluation with this kind of value. Perhaps this is an appropriate equation. Perhaps job evaluation does capture the usefulness of a job to an employer, whatever usefulness may mean. But our advocate goes further and attempts to equate the compensation that is paid for a job with its usefulness to an employer. Here lies the error, for value in use is confused with value in exchange. The compensation an employer pays for a job is truly different from its usefulness to him, just as the price we would normally pay for a glass of water is different from its usefulness to us. The fundamental fact is that labor is exchanged for money. Whatever the usefulness of that labor, its price is a separate question.

I know this distinction is difficult to accept, and I suspect the reason for the difficulty is the language we commonly use in talking about the issues. For example, suppose you need to hire a baby-sitter. The going rate for teenagers is $1.50 an hour; the rate for grandmothers is $3.50. If your child is six years old, you would probably say the teenager was good enough; if your child is six weeks old, you would likely prefer the grandmother. What if your child is one year old? You might very well ask youself, Is the grandmother really worth $2.00 an hour more than the teenager? It may seem as though you are evaluating the worth of the job. After all, you are trying to decide whether the job requires the skill and experience a grandmother has and a teenager lacks. In fact, however, you are establishing your demand for baby-sitting services. You could decide, for instance, that you need the grandmother, but will use her fewer hours than you would have used the teenager.

Now let me change the example and come at my point from another angle. I was talking to Ronald Ehrenberg the other day, and he said he estimated that the price in town for a youngster to mow a lawn is about $4.00 an hour, but the price for a baby-sitter is about $1.50. And then, Ehrenberg, who is a respected economist, added, "It's strange, when you think about it, because your children are a lot more important to you than your lawn." He knew I was interested in comparable worth, so I suspect he was teasing me. But who could disagree that children are more important than lawns? Once again, the way we talk obscures the simple facts that there are plenty of baby-sitters available for $1.50 an hour, but a youngster will not cut your grass for less than $4.00 an hour.

The wages employers pay secretaries, teachers, and electricians are determined in the same way the wages you and I pay baby-sitters and grass cutters are determined. In our free market society, the price of labor is a function of supply and demand. We think this system is democratic because no worker is forced to supply his labor unless he is willing to accept the price an employer offers, and no employer is forced to provide a job unless he is willing to pay the price a worker will accept. Comparable worth is completely alien to this philosophy because comparable worth makes the price of a job depend on someone's value judgments. To impose those judgments on employers and workers alike is to deprive them of the freedom they—we—now enjoy to decide for ourselves how much our labor is worth.

Price also allocates resources in our society. If industry needs more engineers, the price paid for engineers' labor will rise, and people will be attracted to engineering as an occupation. If a surplus of engineers develops, the price paid for engineers' labor will decline relative to other occupations, and some engineers will leave the field and fewer students will study engineering in school. Comparable worth would freeze the relative pay of workers and thus interfere with price as the means of allocating resources.

To elaborate on an example suggested by Vernon Briggs, suppose job evaluation rates equally the jobs of high school mathematics and foreign language teachers. Such ratings are not implausible. The jobs could easily call for equal time in preparation, in class, and in grading; the numbers of students taught could be approximately the same; and the level of skills required could be substantially similar. It would follow that, seniority and other things being equal, mathematics and foreign language teachers should be paid the same. Now suppose a new industry develops a need for workers with the skills possessed by high school mathematics teachers. How will the industry attract them? The most obvious way would be to raise the pay for mathematicians, but this step would create a problem: if the industry were bound by comparable worth, the pay of one job could not be increased unless the pay of all equally and higher rated jobs is also increased. Suppose that mathematicians are rated at 196 points, electrical engineers are rated at 198 points, and department heads are rated at 202 points. If the short supply of mathematicians drives the price of their labor above the pay of electrical engineers and department heads, comparable worth would require increases for these jobs as well, even though the supply of workers for these jobs is plentiful at the lower rates. The inefficiency is obvious.

The school will have similar problems. When the industry offers higher pay for mathematicians, the school will have to decide whether to match the industry's offer or to hold the line on its salary structure. If the school holds the line, the school will lose its mathematics teachers and be unable to replace them or be forced to settle for less qualified replacements. Either way, the quality of education will decline. If the school matches the industry's offer, the school will also have to raise the pay of equally rated foreign language teachers—and the pay of any higher rated teachers and, of course, the pay of all administrators, who are always (but, I might add, rarely with cause) rated above teachers. When teachers and administrators become more costly, the school will employ fewer of them, cut the budgets of other programs, or raise taxes. Whatever the school does, the quality of education will suffer relative to its cost.

These inefficiencies of comparable worth are obvious, but there is something more to fear than inefficiency. The greater risk is government intervention to set pay within firms and to allocate workers across firms. Government would eventually set pay within firms because the drive for equality that underlies the movement for comparable worth could not tolerate the variety of job ratings that would exist otherwise. If firm A rated machine operators above secretaries and secretaries above custodians, but firm B rated these jobs in a different order, charges of discrimination would be inevitable. The only acceptable solution would be a national job evaluation plan, and only the government could manage such a plan. Then the government would be forced to allocate workers across firms because, if prices cannot allocate resources, people will have to do it. Schools and industries will probably not bid against each other for mathematicians because the cost of raising the pay of all employees with equal and higher ratings would be prohibitive. Instead, interested parties will ask the government to decide who gets how many mathematicians this year, and the government will rise to the occasion. And if the government realizes there are too few mathematicians to serve the national interest, the inevitable next step will be action to increase the supply of mathematicians. Comparable worth precludes using higher pay to attract people to occupations. The alternative is to push people into occupations. The push could be subtle, for example, by educational subsidies; or the push could be direct, for example, by outright draft. But however the push is accomplished, the loss to our liberties would be undeniable—and unacceptable. The gain in equality that comparable worth would generate is simply not worth the loss of human freedom that would result.

I realize I cannot prove the government will take over pricing and allocating labor if comparable worth is successful, but I can point to an instructive case. In a country in which comparable worth has apparently raised the pay of women's jobs, namely Australia, wages are set by a national agency.[91] I would hate to see that in this country.

ADVOCATE George Orwell could not have painted a bleaker picture—or a falser one. Our critic's tactic is to complicate things. I will simplify them, and the merits of comparable worth will be apparent.

First, job evaluation plans that are biased against women's jobs must be rectified. Compensable factors have to be chosen so as to recognize the worth of women's work as well as the worth of men's work. Maybe our critic is correct. Maybe all job evaluation is crazy because it disregards market forces. All I am asking is that it be as crazy for men as it is for women.

CRITIC Sometimes it is! For example, the male jobs of civil engineer and petroleum engineer could well receive equal ratings in a job evaluation scheme, but the petroleum engineer would command the higher salary.

ADVOCATE Now who is generalizing from a single case?

CRITIC   There are others—

ADVOCATE   Yes, and there are also inequities across women's jobs; and probably the inequities across men's jobs cancel out the inequities across women's jobs. But when all the canceling is done, the earnings gap remains as proof that most of the inequities are between the sexes, not within them. The basic task is to design job evaluation so that it does not carry the sex discrimination that is rampant in the marketplace into the firm. A break in the vicious circle has to be made somewhere. This is the right place to do it. And if in the process we eliminate the intrasex inequities, such as between civil and petroleum engineers, so much the better.

I do not want the government to dictate which jobs people should hold. I am in favor of the free market system. But the market is not free for women, and it will not become free until it is forced to swallow some pretty strong medicine like comparable worth.

MODERATOR   What is the likelihood that comparable worth will be adopted? Does either of you think it will be ordered by law?

CRITIC   God save us if it is! Our advocate was certainly right in saying that comparable worth is strong medicine—I think this medicine would be worse than the disease.

ADVOCATE   Naturally you would say that. Have you ever suffered from the disease? Or do you benefit because others suffer from it? Many people think a law would not be so bad. More than eighty member-nations of the International Labour Organisation have ratified Convention 100, which encourages members to adopt and apply to all workers "the principle of equal remuneration for men and women workers for work of equal value," and Canada has adopted comparable worth for federal employees.

CRITIC   Fortunately, there is virtually no prospect that comparable worth will be imposed on American employers. Certainly Congress has shown no signs of moving in that direction, and the courts have rejected nearly every case.

The issue first arose as Congress considered the bills that preceded the Equal Pay Act of 1963. The bills introduced in 1961 and 1962 would have prohibited an employer from paying men and women different wages "for work of comparable character on jobs the performance of which requires comparable skills." This language was understood to embrace the concept of comparable worth, and it was endorsed by the Kennedy administration because it believed the economic worth of different jobs could be determined by applying job evaluation systems. Fortunately, Congress was better advised. Representative Katharine St. George moved to substitute the word *equal* for the word *comparable* because the latter word lacked specific meaning and would give too much latitude to the secretary of labor, who would enforce the law. Representative Phil Landrum also feared the prospect that the minions of government would go "trooping around all over the country . . . harassing business with their various interpretations of the term, 'comparable.' . . ." Over the objection of Representative Herbert Zelenko that St. George's amendment would cut out a central element of the administration's proposal, the amendment was adopted. The Senate passed a version of the equal pay bill that also contained the St. George amendment, but because of a conflict between two House committees, the Eighty-seventh Congress adjourned without enacting a bill.[92]

By 1963, the debate between *equal* or *comparable* was settled. The bills in the Eighty-eighth Congress incorporated the St. George amendment. One of these bills was H.R. 6060, which eventually became the Equal Pay Act. It was introduced by Representative Charles Goodell, whose intent on comparable worth was unmistakable.

> *I think it is important that we have clear legislative history on this point. Last year when the House changed the word "comparable" to "equal" the clear intention was to narrow the whole concept. We went from "comparable" to "equal" meaning that the jobs involved should be virtually identical, that is they would be very much alike or closely related to each other.*
>
> *We do not expect the Labor Department people to go into an establishment and attempt to rate jobs that are not equal. We do not want to hear the Department say, "Well, they amount to the same thing," and evaluate them so they come up to the same skill or point.[93]*

This clear intent is reflected in the language of the Equal Pay Act, which outlaws pay differentials only when men and women do "equal work on jobs the performance of which requires equal skill, effort, and responsibility, and which are performed under similar working conditions." The courts have consistently recognized this intent, and comparable worth claims have always failed under the Equal Pay Act, as I am sure our advocate will agree.[94]

ADVOCATE   No, I do not agree that comparable worth claims always fail under the Equal Pay Act, and I do not agree that the issue of comparable worth first arose in 1961. In fact, claims that women are underpaid date back at least to World War II, and at that time the claims met a friendlier welcome. In a case I mentioned earlier, *General Electric Co. and Westinghouse Electric Corp.*, the War Labor Board entertained a claim brought by a union that the employers compensated jobs customarily performed by women less, on a comparative content basis, than jobs customarily performed by men.[95] The chairman of the board, Lloyd Garrison, relied on George Taylor's characterization of the issue in earlier board cases. In one involving General Motors, Taylor said,

It is claimed that the rate of that job classification always performed by women is out of line with the rate of other job classifications. The problem then is no different from any other occupational rate question. The claim is actually that a job rate is out of line with other rates, and it doesn't matter who performs the work. . . . In all such cases, it is a question of job evaluation to determine whether or not an intra-plant inequality exists.[96]

In another case involving the Bendix Aviation Corporation, Taylor said,

The problem presented in this case is not primarily related to the Board's policy on equal pay for equal work to female employees. On the contrary, it represents a fundamental problem of intra-plant wage relationships arising from a lack of balance between various rates.

What is obviously needed in this situation is a reevaluation of job classifications on the basis of job content.[97]

Relying on these and other precedents, the board announced two principles: First, when men and women performed different jobs, it was presumed that differing rates of compensation were appropriate. Second, the presumption could be overcome by evidence "derived from a comparison of the content of the jobs [performed by women] with the content of the jobs performed by men." The presumption was overcome in the *General Electric and Westinghouse* case by evidence about the employees' jobs, and the union won the case for the women.

CRITIC   Fortunately for the economy, the jurisdiction of the War Labor Board expired in 1945. Also, I believe—and I know our advocate will correct me if I am mistaken—that the board generally did not dictate to the parties what the rates of pay should be. Instead, the board typically ordered the parties to negotiate an adjustment.[98]

ADVOCATE   Yes, but if the parties could not agree, the case would go to arbitration, so there is precedent for referring comparable worth claims to neutral third parties like arbitrators—or judges.[99]

As for comparable worth under the Equal Pay Act, the courts have recognized from the outset that equal work does not mean identical work. It is sufficient that the men's and women's work be substantially equal.[100] Moreover, the judges have been willing to compare not only the specific tasks performed, but also the value of the tasks. In *Hodgson* v. *Brookhaven General Hospital,* the court was called upon to decide whether male orderlies and female nurses' aides performed equal work in light of evidence that the orderlies were assigned some tasks not assigned to aides. The court held the appropriate standard was whether the additional tasks

(1) require extra effort, (2) consume a significant amount of time of all those whose pay differentials are to be justified in terms of them, and (3) are of an economic value commensurate with the pay differential.[101]

Clearly, if the economic value of the additional tasks is less than the value of the shared tasks, the additional tasks cannot explain a pay differential.

The economic value of additional tasks determined the outcome of *Shultz* v. *Wheaton Glass Co.,* in which there were male and female selector-packers. The men were paid $2.35 an hour, the women $2.14 an hour. There was another category of employees, snap-up boys, who performed miscellaneous unskilled labor for $2.16 an hour. When the employer tried to justify the pay differential between male and female selector-packers by arguing that the men occasionally had to perform the work of snap-up boys, the court pointed to the wages of snap-up boys and concluded that the value of their work could not explain the differential. Even though the men may have spent as much as 18 percent of their time doing snap-up work, which involved sixteen tasks not performed by women, "there would be no rational explanation why men who at times perform work paying two cents per hour more than their female counterparts should for that reason receive 21½ cents per hour more than females for the work they do in common."[102]

Another case in which a court took account of the value of work is *Wetzel* v. *Liberty Mutual,* in which an insurance company violated the Equal Pay Act by employing male claims adjusters and female claims representatives and paying the men about 50 percent more than the women. The jobs were not identical. For example, the women handled a higher volume of cases, but the men handled cases involving higher claims. The men traveled to appointments; the women stayed in the office. Yet the court decided the jobs demanded equal work and, in reaching this decision, relied heavily on the testimony of an industrial psychologist who applied a factor point job evaluation plan to the jobs.[103]

I think these cases hold out the promise that claims of comparable worth may be proved under the Equal Pay Act, provided the jobs are fairly similar in content.

CRITIC   And I think not. Note that in all of those cases, the courts found the jobs were equal, though not every task was identical. Male and female selector-packers did basically the same work; so did male orderlies and female nurses' aides and claims adjusters and claims representatives. The Equal Pay Act has never been, and should never be, stretched to reach cases in which the jobs are significantly different. Nor should Title VII be stretched to cases of genuinely different jobs.

It is important to keep in mind that the Eighty-eighth Congress passed both the Equal Pay Act and Title VII. I cannot believe that the very same representatives and senators who purposefully excluded comparable worth from the Equal Pay Act in 1963 suddenly and silently changed their minds and incorporated comparable worth into Title VII in 1964. In fact, I believe the Bennett Amendment is proof positive that Congress meant to exclude comparable worth from Title VII.

The Bennett Amendment was offered late during the Senate debates, but the issue of the relationship of the Equal Pay Act and Title VII had arisen earlier. Senator Joseph Clark, one of the floor managers of Title VII, placed in the *Congressional Record* a memorandum he had prepared to answer objections to this title. One objection was that Title VII did not include the limitations carefully built into the Equal Pay Act. Senator Clark replied, "The standards in the Equal Pay Act for determining discrimination as to wages . . . are applicable to the comparable situation under Title VII."[104] But Senator Wallace Bennett was not satisfied, especially because sex had been added as a protected class to Title VII with comparatively little debate, and he proposed the following amendment:

It shall not be an unlawful employment practice under this title for an employer to differentiate upon the basis of sex in determining the amount of wages or compensation paid or to be paid to employees if such differentiation is authorized by the provisions of section 6(d) of the Fair Labor Standards Act, as amended [the Equal Pay Act].[105]

The intent of this amendment was clearly to ensure that Senator Clark's interpretation was written into the statute. Indeed, Senator Bennett himself said, "The purpose of my amendment is to provide that in the event of conflicts, the provisions of the Equal Pay Act shall not be nullified. I understand that the leadership in charge of this bill have agreed to the amendment as a proper technical correction of the bill."[106] The leadership of the House also agreed to accept the Bennett Amendment. Representative Emmanuel Celler, chairman of the House Judiciary Committee and a leading sponsor of the civil rights bill, explained to his colleagues that the amendment "[p]rovides that compliance with the Fair Labor Standards Act as amended satisfies the requirement of the title barring discrimination because of sex. . . ."[107] Thus everyone understood that the decision on comparable worth reflected in the Equal Pay Act would not be overturned by Title VII.

ADVOCATE   Everyone but the Supreme Court! This very issue was decided by the Court in 1981 in *County of Washington* v. *Gunther.* In that case, a county employed male guards and female matrons in its jail and paid the men more than the women. The men spent most of their time guarding prisoners, while the women guarded fewer prisoners and devoted substantial time to clerical duties. Thus, the women's Equal Pay Act claim was rejected because the women's job was different from the men's. But the women also sought to prove a claim of comparable worth under Title VII. They offered to introduce evidence that the county had conducted a survey of jobs in the community to determine the prevailing wages for work similar to the guards' and the matrons' and that the county paid the guards the prevailing wage for their work but purposefully paid the matrons less than the prevailing wage. The county objected that this evidence was irrelevant because Congress intended that claims of sex discrimination in compensation would be governed exclusively by the Equal Pay Act—just as our critic has argued. By the time the case worked its way up to the Supreme Court, the issue had been narrowed to this very question, whether Title VII as applied to claims of sex discrimination in compensation is any broader than the Equal Pay Act.

And the Court clearly held that Title VII is broader than the Equal Pay Act. The Court looked at four sources that could shed light on the intent of Congress. One was the Equal Employment Opportunity Commission, which was unfortunately no help because it had taken both sides of the issue at different times. Another source was the policy underlying Title VII. This policy pointed toward a broad reading of the statute; otherwise, many kinds of discrimination would go unremedied. For example, said the Court, "if an employer hired a woman for a unique position in the company and then admitted that her salary would have been higher had she been male, the woman would be unable to obtain legal redress" under a narrow reading of the act. The third source to which the Court referred was the legislative history of the Bennett Amendment. Our critic is right that the amendment was considered to be a technical modification, but the Court held the amendment was meant to protect the administration of the Equal Pay Act, not to narrow the scope of Title VII. The fourth source to which the Court turned was the language of the amendment itself, which our critic chose to gloss over.

The amendment exempts from Title VII any practice authorized by the Equal Pay Act. Obviously, the critical word is *authorized.* If this word were construed to mean *permitted,* that is, *not outlawed,* any practice beyond the reach of the Equal Pay Act would be lawful under Title VII. But

the Court rejected this interpretation because it would condone too many wrongful kinds of discriminatory behavior,
such as the one in which the employer tells a woman he
would pay her more if she were a man. Instead, the Court
construed *authorized* in its ordinary sense of "to empower;
to give a right or authority to act." In this sense, the Equal
Pay Act authorizes only practices that fall within its four
defenses. Those defenses allow an employer to pay one sex
more than another if the differential "is made pursuant to
(i) a seniority system; (ii) a merit system; (iii) a system which
measures earnings by quantity or quality of production; or
(iv) a differential based on any other factor other than sex."
It follows that the Bennett Amendment was meant to ensure
that Title VII would not override the defenses to the Equal
Pay Act. The amendment was not meant to restrict Title
VII in any other way.

CRITIC   Our advocate is right to assert the Supreme Court
held in *Gunther* that the Bennett Amendment does not limit
claims of sex discrimination in compensation brought under
Title VII to the requirements of the Equal Pay Act. However, our advocate is wrong to assert the Court held the
amendment was not meant to restrict Title VII in any way
beyond the four defenses to the Equal Pay Act. The Court
expressly refrained from holding that, if the matrons' evidence were true, they would establish a violation of Title
VII. In its own words, the Court said, "We are not called
upon in this case to decide whether [the matrons] have stated
a prima facie case of sex discrimination . . . or to lay down
standards for the further conduct of this litigation." Even
more important is what the Court said directly about comparable worth.

*We emphasize at the outset the narrowness of the question
before us in this case. [The matrons'] claim is not based on the
controversial concept of "comparable worth," under which plain-*

tiffs might claim increased compensation on the basis of a comparison of the intrinsic worth or difficulty of their job with that of other jobs in the same organization or community. Rather, [the matrons] seek to prove, by direct evidence, that their wages were depressed because of intentional sex discrimination, consisting of setting the wage scale of female guards, but not for male guards, at a level lower than [the county's] own survey of outside markets and the worth of the jobs warranted.

Later the Court again expressed its reluctance to get involved with comparable worth.

[This] suit does not require a court to make its own subjective assessment of the value of the male and female guard jobs, or to attempt by statistical technique or other method to quantify the effect of sex discrimination on the wage rates.[108]

It is evident the Supreme Court wants nothing to do with comparable worth.

ADVOCATE   I am prepared to agree that *Gunther* is more important for what it did not do than for what it did do. If the Supreme Court had held the Bennett Amendment made Title VII and the Equal Pay Act congruent with regard to claims of sex discrimination in compensation, that would have been the end of comparable worth. The Court could have killed comparable worth aborning, but did not, and so the issue is still alive in the courts.

CRITIC   Alive, but not well. In the first place, the federal courts of appeals that have ruled squarely on comparable worth have held against women. Consider the leading Tenth Circuit case of *Lemons* v. *City and County of Denver*, in which the city compensated its employees by reference to the pay scales for analogous jobs in the surrounding community. City-employed nurses, who were paid on a par with nurses in the private sector, sued "because their work has not been properly recognized and because nurses have almost universally been women." In other words, the women claimed the labor market discriminated against women's work, and the employer's compensation system incorporated that discrimination. "[T]he plaintiffs urge that the City should not mirror this condition which prevails in the community and so perpetuate it. . . ." The court conceded that the "relationship of pay for nurses to pay for other positions is obviously a product of past attitudes, practices, and perhaps of supply and demand," but nevertheless held, "This type of disparity was not sought to be adjusted by the Civil Rights Act. . . . The courts under existing authority cannot require the City within its employment practices to reassess the worth of services in each position in relation to all others, and to strike a new balance and relationship."[109]

Similar facts were presented in even more dramatic fashion to the Eighth Circuit in *Christensen* v. *State of Iowa.* A state university used to determine the wage scales for its jobs by reference to the wages paid for similar work in the local labor market. Then in 1974 the university instituted a new compensation system under which jobs were placed in labor grades according to an objective evaluation of each job's relative worth to the employer, regardless of the going rates in the labor market. The pay range for each labor grade was determined by reference to the market rates for similar jobs. Here a hitch developed. The new system—which was obviously a form of job evaluation—placed clerical jobs and physical plant jobs in the same labor grade. The hitch was that the price paid for physical plant jobs (including electricians, carpenters, and plumbers) was higher in the labor market than the price paid for clerical jobs (including telephone operators, mail clerks, and typists). Accordingly, the university had to improve the pay of starting physical plant employees, but not of starting clerical employees. It hardly needs mentioning that, although jobs in both departments were open to employees of either sex, nearly all physical plant employees were men, while all clerical employees were women. Therefore, the effect of the university's deviations from its compensation system was to pay men more than women for equally rated jobs. The women sued under Title VII and lost. The court's opinion is particularly instructive.

[The women] contend that [the university's] policy violates Title VII by perpetuating wage differences resulting from past discrimination. They argue that long-standing discriminatory practices in the local job market, which channeled women workers into a small number of jobs, resulted in an over-supply of workers and depressed wages in these jobs. Therefore [the university's] reliance in part upon prevailing wage rates in determining beginning pay scales for jobs of equal worth to the university serves to carry over the effects of sex discrimination in the market-place into the wage policies of the college.

This argument misconstrues the purposes of Title VII. The federal policy embodied in Title VII is that individuals shall be entitled to equal opportunities in employment on the basis of fitness and without discrimination. . . .

Equality of opportunity is not at issue here. Instead, [the women] seek a construction of Title VII that may establish a prima facie violation of that Act whenever employees of different sexes receive disparate compensation for work of differing skills that may, subjectively, be of equal value to the employer, but does not command an equal price in the labor market. [This] theory ignores economic realities. The value of the job to the employer represents but one factor affecting wages. Other factors may include the supply of workers willing to do the job and the ability of the workers to band together to bargain collectively for higher wages. We find nothing in the text and history of Title VII sug-

gesting that Congress intended to abrogate the laws of supply and demand or other economic principles that determine wage rates for various kinds of work. We do not interpret Title VII as requiring an employer to ignore the market in setting wage rates for genuinely different classifications.[110]

Finally, I would like to discuss the Ninth Circuit's opinions in *Gunther*. The Supreme Court decided only one of the issues raised in the lower courts. Another issue, on which the Supreme Court did not rule but the court of appeals did, was whether the matrons could win their case merely by proving that their job was worth as much to the county as the guards' job was worth. The answer was no. The court held that, if a Title VII plaintiff tries to prove wage discrimination

based solely on a comparison of the work she performs, she will have to show that her job requirements are substantially equal, not comparable, to that of a similarly situated male. The standards developed under the Equal Pay Act are relevant in this inquiry. . . . [B]ecause a comparable work standard cannot be substituted for an equal work standard, evidence of comparable work, although not necessarily irrelevant in proving discrimination under some alternative theory, will not alone be sufficient to establish a prima facie case.[111]

The weight of authority is heavily against comparable worth in the courts.

ADVOCATE   While I cannot say comparable worth has been received with open arms by the judiciary, I would like to discuss a persuasive Third Circuit case that has taken a more enlightened view of the issue. In *IUE* v. *Westinghouse,* the plaintiffs alleged the employer formerly segregated jobs by sex. In 1939 a wage administration manual was promulgated. The manual said points had been assigned to jobs based on the knowledge, training, demands, and responsibilities of the jobs and then, based on the points awarded them, jobs were slotted in labor grades. Finally, pay was determined for the labor grades. In short, it was alleged the employer used a job evaluation plan to establish compensation. The plaintiffs then contended that wages for female jobs were deliberately set lower than the wages for male jobs in the same labor grades. In other words, female jobs were paid less than male jobs with the same point scores. The 1939 manual expressly stated, "The rate or range for Labor Grades [for women] do not coincide with the values on the men's scale. Basically then, we have another wage curve . . . for women below and not parallel with the men's curve." In 1965 the employer ceased designating jobs as male or female, abandoned separate wage scales for men and women, and adopted a new unitary wage scale for all employees. Still, ten years later the formerly female jobs were staffed predominately by women, and the formerly male jobs were staffed predominately by men. Furthermore, the new scale, claimed the plaintiffs, purposefully carried forward the discrimination of the old dual scales because formerly female jobs that in the past had been placed in the same labor grades as men's jobs were suddenly placed in labor grades beneath the men's jobs. So once again women were paid less than men for work of equal value.

The focus of the parties' arguments and the court's opinion was the Bennett Amendment, which we need not discuss because the Supreme Court settled that issue in *Gunther*. Nevertheless, I want to point out that the *Westinghouse* court saw an important analogy between sex discrimination and other forms of discrimination: "The statutory issue here is whether Congress intended to permit Westinghouse to willfully discriminate against women in a way in which it could not discriminate against blacks or whites, Jews or Gentiles, Protestants or Catholics, Italians or Irishmen, or any other group protected by [Title VII]."[112] The Supreme Court relied on the same analogy in *Los Angeles* v. *Manhart*, a case involving sex discrimination in pension funds. The Court said that "a statute that was designed to make race irrelevant in the employment market . . . could not reasonably be construed to permit a take-home-pay differential based on a racial classification."[113] Based on this analogy, the Court held an employer could not require higher pension contributions from female employees than from their male counterparts. Therefore, when the Third Circuit held in *Westinghouse* that Congress intended to protect sex as fully as race, color, religion, and national origin, the court stood on firm ground.[114] If an employer pays a woman less money than a man because of sex, that is just as illegal as paying a black less than a white because of race. The court decided that the plaintiffs' allegations, if proved, would establish a violation of Title VII, and this holding is an important victory for comparable worth.

CRITIC   I disagree that the *Westinghouse* case is a victory for comparable worth—in fact, I do not think it involved comparable worth at all. And I disagree that the issue of the Bennett Amendment is settled. I think *Westinghouse* is very much like *Gunther* because in both cases the plaintiffs were trying to prove their employers intentionally paid women less because of their sex. In *Gunther,* the evidence of intent was the county's disregard of its prevailing wage survey; in *Westinghouse,* the evidence of intent was the employer's reclassification of female jobs into lower pay grades. In neither case did the plaintiffs seek to win solely by proving their jobs were worth as much as men's jobs. When plaintiffs have tried to win on such a narrow showing, as in *Lemons* and *Christensen,* they have lost.

As for the Bennett Amendment, there is a complicated

aspect of the *Gunther* case we have not yet discussed. As our advocate correctly pointed out, the Equal Pay Act allows pay differentials based on a seniority system, a merit system, a system which measures earnings by quantity or quality of production, or any factor other than sex. At the time the Bennett Amendment was proposed, the first three of these exceptions were already part of Title VII—indeed, they were part of the very same section to which the Bennett Amendment was added. The fourth exception was surely implied because, if a pay differential is based on something other than sex, it is not sex discrimination in the first place. It follows that the purpose of the Bennett Amendment was not simply to bring the Equal Pay Act's exceptions into Title VII. The amendment must have had some other purpose. What was the purpose? The Supreme Court's answer was clear: to prohibit claims of comparable worth.

ADVOCATE   What do you base that statement on? Nowhere in the *Gunther* opinion can I find any statement that the Bennett Amendment was meant to prohibit comparable worth.

CRITIC   I concede there is no such direct statement, but the idea is surely implied. The Court went out of its way to emphasize that employers may defend themselves against Equal Pay Act claims by showing that "pay differentials are based on a bona fide use of 'other factors other than sex.'" Immediately after this statement, the Court quoted Representative Goodell's admonition that courts are not permitted under the Equal Pay Act to "substitute their judgment for the judgment of the employer . . . who [has] established and employed a bona fide rating system." Putting these remarks together, the inference is obvious that the Court believes the Bennett Amendment was intended to limit cases of sex discrimination in compensation under Title VII to claims of intentional underpayment, such as the women in *Gunther* itself alleged.[115] But as for the true comparable worth cases—in which women allege their jobs are underpaid because the market undervalues them or a job evaluation system awards them too few points—the Supreme Court wants nothing to do with the issue.

ADVOCATE   Reading between the lines of Supreme Court opinions is risky business, and I am not inclined to join battle with our critic over what the Court meant by what it did not say. But I would like to quote two other statements from the *Gunther* opinion. First this:

As Congress itself has indicated, a "broad approach" to the definition of equal employment opportunity is essential to overcoming and undoing the effect of discrimination. . . . We must therefore avoid interpretations of Title VII that deprive victims of discrimination of a remedy, without clear congressional mandate.

I suggest there is no "clear congressional mandate" permitting employers to underpay certain jobs because they are held by women. Second:

[The county's argument] is thus flatly inconsistent with our past interpretations of Title VII as "prohibit[ing] all practices in whatever form which create inequality in employment opportunity due to discrimination on the basis of race, religion, sex, or national origin". . . . As we said in Los Angeles Department of Water & Power v. Manhart *. . . "In forbidding employers to discriminate against individuals because of their sex, Congress intended to strike at the* entire spectrum *of disparate treatment of men and women resulting from sex stereotypes."*[116]

Underpaying women's work is surely the result of sex stereotypes, such as that women work for pin money or they are less reliable or productive workers than men. But I do not wish to push this language too far. My point is simply that both sides can find support in *Gunther,* and how the Court will rule in future cases is anyone's guess.

CRITIC   True enough, but we need not guess how the lower courts have ruled since the *Gunther* decision was announced. I think *Briggs* v. *City of Madison* is a good example. Public health nurses, who were virtually all women, sued the city because sanitarians, who were all men, were paid more. The prerequisites for being hired into the two jobs were almost identical, and the duties of the jobs were similar as well. In fact, the judge wrote "that the jobs held by [the nurses] required skill, effort, and responsibility at least equal to, and possibly in excess of, that required of sanitarians by their jobs. . . ."[117] Nevertheless, the women lost, and the reasons why are worth repeating.

The women advanced the argument, suggested in a leading law review article,[118] that they can establish a prima facie case under Title VII by proving "(1) they are members of a protected class, (2) who occupy a sex-segregated job classification (3) that is paid less than (4) a sex-segregated classification occupied by men."[119] The theory underlying this argument is similar to the theory our advocate offered earlier in this dialogue: that job segregation and wage discrimination are closely connected because the same forces that determine that women will be limited to specific jobs also determine that the economic value of women's jobs is low. The court rejected this theory, in part because of reasons I have already mentioned (for example, women may choose the jobs they hold because of factors like convenient hours) and in part because the theory focuses exclusively on social and historical facts, instead of on the actions of a given employer. Title VII, after all, imposes liability on employers, and it would be grossly unfair to hold them accountable for others' actions. I think this judge has identified a serious flaw in the push for comparable worth. So long as an employer allows any interested, qualified woman to hold any job—and, following *Gunther,* does not intentionally underpay her because of her sex—it seems terribly unjust to make this employer responsible for the social forces that may limit, or cause women to limit themselves, to lower paying jobs.

ADVOCATE   As usual, our critic tells only half the story. The other and more encouraging half of the story of the *Briggs* case is this: the judge recognized that women could establish a prima facie case under Title VII by proving the four facts our critic mentioned plus one more, namely, that the requirements of the jobs at issue are substantially similar. I think the main reason the judge rejected the women's first argument was his belief that differences in job requirements often account for differences in compensation. Thus, when the nurses proved the additional fact that their job was highly similar to the sanitarians' job, the judge decided they had proved enough to justify a finding of sex discrimination.

CRITIC   Except, of course, that the women lost the case because the employer proved a valid defense: the labor market. The judge believed the testimony of the director of the health department that sanitarians' pay was set higher than nurses' pay in order to attract qualified applicants. When the women argued that this defense allows an employer to benefit from, and help perpetuate, the undervaluation of women's work in the labor market, the judge replied that Title VII limits an employer's liability to his own acts of discrimination.

Nothing in the Act indicates that the employer's liability extends to conditions of the marketplace which it did not create. Nothing indicates that it is improper for an employer to pay the wage rates necessary to compete in the marketplace for qualified individuals. That there may be an abundance of applicants qualified for some jobs and a dearth of skilled applicants for other jobs is not a condition for which a particular employer bears responsibility.[120]

ADVOCATE   I cannot deny that the judge's education is incomplete. I am gratified he has taken an important step in recognizing that a prima facie case of comparable worth can be established under Title VII. I think it will not be long before judges realize that the defense of the labor market is a false defense because the market discriminates against women. But we will take our gains where we find them.

Fortunately, women do not have to rely exclusively on the courts to attain equity in compensation. A number of cities and states have taken important strides in this direction. Fourteen states have laws on the books that can be read to require equal pay for jobs of comparable worth, and others are considering legislation.[121] For example, the law of Massachusetts says:

No employer shall discriminate in any way in the payment of wages as between the sexes, or pay any female in his employ salary or wage rates less than the rates paid to male employees for work of like or comparable character or work on like or comparable operations. . . .[122]

And the law in Kentucky reads:

No employer shall discriminate between employees in the same establishment on the basis of sex, by paying wages to any employee in any occupation in this state at a rate less than the rate

*at which he pays any employee of the opposite sex for comparable
work on jobs which have comparable requirements relating to skill,
effort, and responsibility . . .*[123]

Given the controversy that developed in Congress over the
difference between equal work and comparable work, I think
it is no accident that these and other state statutes use the
word *comparable.*

CRITIC   It may be no accident, but it surely is a serious
mistake. Let me refer back to the study our advocate cited
concerning the State of Washington. Chemists were rated
below nurses, but paid more. Suppose the same evaluation
plan is applied to a private employer, and suppose he cannot
maintain his competitive status by paying both at the chemists' rate, so he pays them both at the lower nurses' rate.
What is he going to do when he cannot attract or retain
chemists? The answer is obvious: he is going to break the law.
He will find a way to get the chemists he needs. He may
provide them with free lunches or long vacations, or he may
pay them under the table. Most likely, he will monkey with
the evaluation plan in order to raise the rating for chemists.
I suppose the nurses will challenge every trick he tries, and
the courts will be inundated with these cases. A law that
ignores reality will itself be ignored. Americans kept right
on drinking after Prohibition, and American employers will
keep right on paying market wages after comparable worth.
    Let me add that, if women are underpaid, the fault is
not entirely employers'. Even our advocate has emphasized
premarket factors like socialization. Comparable worth is
directed at employers, but, to the extent that premarket factors are responsible, it is misdirected. Nothing is going to
stop little Nancy Jones from wanting to be like her mother,
and nothing is going to make Mr. Jones want to teach his
daughter how to repair automobiles.

ADVOCATE   I disagree, and history is on my side. Most Americans, and surely most Southerners, probably agreed with William Graham Sumner when he wrote in 1907 that "legislation cannot make mores" and "stateways cannot change folkways." In other words, no amount of government action could change racial prejudice and discrimination. Half a century later, Dwight David Eisenhower said the same thing when he declined to use federal power vigorously to enforce the Supreme Court's desegregation decisions of the 1950s. But today we know otherwise.

In the first place, there was always a striking contradiction about Sumner's argument: the same people who relied on it as a bulwark against liberalizing legislation had themselves very substantially changed race relations by means of the Jim Crow laws. Between the end of the Civil War and the turn of the century, blacks and whites for the most part worked, traveled, ate, and even lodged in the same accommodations in the South. Then the Jim Crow laws, enacted primarily after 1900, required racial segregation, and obedience to these laws changed behavior.[124] Segregation in the South was a phenomenon of the first half of the twentieth century, and the law played a leading role in creating and maintaining that phenomenon.

By the same token, desegregation has been a phenomenon of the second half of the twentieth century, and the law has played a leading role in this phenomenon as well. There is no doubt that the civil rights acts of the 1950s and 1960s have changed Americans' behavior toward minorities and women in the past quarter century. Attitudes have also changed, though perhaps more than the law has been at work here. Employers may resist comparable worth now, but once it is clearly the law, they will find ways to live with it. We must not be deterred from doing what is right merely because some individuals consider themselves to be above the law.

CRITIC   It is not a matter of being above the law. It is a matter of economic survival. If an employer cannot hire chemists at the legal rate, he will hire them at an illegal rate, or he will go out of business. In fact, the more willing an employer is to break the law, that is, the more he is prepared to get the chemists he needs, the more his business will prosper. Respect for law is not particularly high in America today, and comparable worth will reduce whatever legitimacy the law may have.

ADVOCATE   I recognize there will be problems at the outset. I suppose the first employers who were willing to hire black workers had similar problems. The answer is to apply the law simultaneously to all employers in an evenhanded way.

CRITIC   Easier said than done!

MODERATOR   Does either of you think it possible that comparable worth will be implemented through collective bargaining?

ADVOCATE   I think there is a strong possibility that collective bargaining will lead to pay equity. Perhaps my strongest reasons for saying this are two simple statistics: organized women workers earn from 20 to 46 percent more than unorganized women workers, and the proportion of union members who are women is steadily increasing.[125] Also, in 1979 the AFL–CIO convention adopted a resolution supporting comparable worth and urging its affiliates "to adopt the concept of equal pay for equal work of comparable value in organizing and in negotiating collective bargaining agreements."[126] And the Coalition of Labor Union Women (CLUW), which was founded in 1974 and now has more than eight thousand members representing sixty-five international unions, has assigned comparable worth to a top priority.[127]

Of course, collective bargaining is performed by individual unions, not by associations like the AFL-CIO and CLUW. I am glad to say that several major unions have brought comparable worth to the bargaining table. One of the leaders is the American Federation of State, County, and Municipal Employees (AFSCME), which represented city employees who went on strike over comparable worth in San Jose, California, in 1981. A study by an independent consultant had revealed that the city paid on average 15 percent less for women's jobs than for comparable men's jobs. The contract was settled by providing for a total pay increase to the city's two thousand employees of $4.80 million over two years; $1.45 million—more than 30 percent—of this settlement was reserved for raising the pay of underpaid women.[128] I think that is a remarkable victory for women.

Other unions have been active, too: the International Union of Electrical Workers (IUE) has filed several lawsuits, including *Gunther*. The Communication Workers of America (CWA) has raised comparable worth with the Bell System. The United Electrical Workers (UE) as early as 1970 in its contract with General Electric sacrificed money from a general pay increase in order to give an extra boost to women's jobs at the lower end of the scale. The list goes on.[129]

CRITIC   I have much less objection to a union's attempts to raise the pay of a certain job than I do to a judge's order that pay be raised based on some vague notion of the inherent worth of a job. I am confident that an employer at the bargaining table will keep his self-interest in mind and refuse to accept irrational demands. If secretaries are making $5.00 an hour and a union comes in with a demand for $7.50, but the employer knows the going rate is $5.25 and competitors are paying $5.25, I am fairly sure the employer will hold the line. If not, the market will give the firm what it deserves.

But I wonder what comparable worth will do to unions. If they become deeply committed to it, I am afraid it might be a divisive issue. Frankly, I doubt unions really are deeply committed to comparable worth. For example, my reading of the San Jose strike is that some opportunists took advantage of public ignorance to make themselves look good in the newspapers. Comparable worth really had nothing to do with the strike, because both the city and the union agreed from the very start that substantial sums should be set aside for raising the pay of women's jobs. The real cause of the strike was that the city offered an across-the-board increase of 6 percent for two years, while the union wanted a four-year contract with 10 percent in the first year and cost-of-living increases thereafter. The final settlement was a compromise: a two-year contract with about 8 percent increases each year for all jobs. As for comparable worth, the settlement provided $1.45 million above the 8 percent to adjust the pay of women's jobs; but that is the same amount the city offered for this purpose at the start of negotiations, and it is the same amount that was in the tentative contract whose rejection led to the strike.[130] So whatever the parties said and however the press sensationalized it, the union did not strike over comparable worth.

ADVOCATE   I think it is significant that a union bargained for and won a very substantial sum of money to be used exclusively to raise the pay of women's jobs. The union could have put the entire settlement into an equal percentage increase for all jobs, which is exactly what would have happened ten years ago. Whether or not the strike was precipitated by comparable worth is beside the point.

CRITIC   I think the real cause of the strike is exactly the point, because I do not think the labor movement is as firmly committed to comparable worth as our advocate implies. It is no coincidence that the mayor and a majority of the city council of San Jose were women. The politicians wanted comparable worth at least as much as the union.

Comparable worth is like seniority and pensions and vacations and many other issues that cross the bargaining table: they can all divide a union internally. Older workers want protection for seniority; younger workers prefer merit and ability. Workers with families want insurance plans; single workers want take-home pay. Higher paid workers want percentage increases; lower paid workers want straight dollar increases. Comparable worth divides men from women in a highly visible way. In a decade in which give-backs have become a reality and a union does well to hold the line—let alone to keep up with inflation—I doubt that men are going to stand by quietly while their income is eroded in order to make raises for women.

In fact, I think employers may use comparable worth to weaken the labor movement. There is a strong antiunion movement afoot in the country today. Many employers who have dealt with unions for years are looking for ways to break off those dealings, and employers whose workers are unorganized are willing to go to great lengths to maintain a union-free environment. I think such employers can easily use comparable worth to drive a wedge down the middle of a union. All an employer has to say is, "I have *x* dollars this year for a new contract. If you want to raise the pay of women's work by 25 percent, raises for men's work will have to be limited to 2 percent." What is that going to do to politics inside a union?

I will make one last point about the problems comparable worth will cause unions. So far, I have discussed the employer who deals with a single union. Many employers have several union contracts. If one of those unions goes on a rampage for comparable worth, the others may have to get involved to keep their members happy, and that is going to lead to some very complex bargaining. It seems likely to me that some unions will care more about comparable worth than others, and that may put heavy pressure on union solidarity.

ADVOCATE   I acknowledge that comparable worth would be easier to bargain for if the economy were stronger, and I know that unscrupulous employers have always looked for ways to divide unions and to set members against each other. But I also know that unions have found ways to deal with these problems. Unions have accommodated the interests of older and younger members, married and single members, skilled and unskilled members. I think unions will find ways—some unions already have found ways—to deal with comparable worth. For example, raising the pay of women's jobs is not the only way to achieve pay equity. Another strategy is to restructure jobs so that more men and women can perform the same jobs and earn the same pay. Suppose there are twenty jobs on an assembly line, and each job has eight tasks. A man or a woman could perform seven of the tasks, but one requires the worker to lift a hundred pounds once an hour. Structured in this way, these jobs are likely to be men's jobs because not many women can handle that much weight. Now suppose that the jobs—not the assembly line, just the jobs—are restructured so that nineteen of them require the seven tasks a man or a woman can perform, and one job is assigned all of the lifting for the other nineteen. Result: an awful lot of pay equity for women at no loss of pay to men. I think working men will respond to the injustice their sisters in the union are suffering, and the labor movement will be stronger for it.

CRITIC   And I think not. It is no coincidence that the unions our advocate has identified as leaders in the movement for comparable worth—AFSCME, CWA, and the electrical workers' organizations—represent large numbers of women. The IBEW's membership is 30 percent female; the IUE and AFSCME are 40 percent female; and 51 percent of CWA's members are women.[131] These numbers are understandable because women are concentrated in jobs offered by the industries with which these unions negotiate: in manufacturing of electrical machinery, equipment, and supplies, 40 percent of all workers are women; in government, 43 percent of workers are women; and in the telephone and telegraph industry, 47 percent of workers are women.[132] Comparable worth is a big issue for these unions because women are a big part of these unions.

But women are not a big part of most other unions. In fact, 45 percent of all female unionists belong to only twenty-six national unions. Almost 60 percent of all national unions have less than 20 percent female memberships, and 70 percent of all national unions have less than 30 percent female memberships. I seriously doubt that comparable worth will be important for the overwhelming majority of American unions. But even if I am wrong and all unions go all out for comparable worth, the total effect will be more cosmetic than substantive, for barely 12 percent of working women are organized.[133]

ADVOCATE   Our critic forgets how gains won by unions radiate to the benefit of unorganized workers.

CRITIC   And our advocate forgets that organized women already earn substantially more than unorganized women. Those gains have apparently not radiated.

MODERATOR   A brief summary from each side is now in order. Our advocate has the burden of convincing us that change is appropriate and is therefore entitled to the last word. So we will begin with our critic.

CRITIC   I can hardly summarize all my arguments, but I can repeat my most important points. First, there is little or no hard evidence that the earnings gap is caused by discrimination in the labor market. In fact, much of the gap plainly results from causes outside the market. Many extramarket causes are legitimate, such as the choice women freely make to become mothers and keep house. If other extramarket causes are not legitimate, it is certainly unfair to make an innocent employer pay for discrimination over which the firm has no control.

   Second, a job has no inherent worth. A job has only a market value. Even job evaluation does not pretend to measure the real worth of a job. Instead, job evaluation, as it is practiced today, relies on the market to establish the pay of key jobs. Job evaluation is a useful device for approximating the market value of unique jobs for which market rates do not exist, but job evaluation could never substitute for the labor market.

   Third, if the labor market is functioning improperly

with respect to certain jobs, the right answer is to correct the imperfection, not subvert the market. For example, if women are excluded from high-paying jobs or paid less than men for equal work, we should vigorously enforce Title VII and the Equal Pay Act. Under no circumstances should we abandon the market as the institution that prices and allocates labor. If the market were abandoned, terrible inefficiencies would surely result, and the government would soon step in and create worse problems than we have now.

Fourth, Title VII was meant to guarantee equality of opportunities, not equality of outcomes, and comparable worth is no part of this guarantee. The Congress that rejected comparable worth in 1963 did not embrace it in 1964.

Finally, I want to emphasize that comparable worth is an issue of interests, not of rights. Women simply want more money for the work they do. I do not blame them for that; I would like more money for the work I do, too. But as long as women are free to become plumbers and prefer to become secretaries instead, they have no right to demand plumbers' pay for secretaries' work.

ADVOCATE   I, too, will limit myself to the main points. The first is that there is ample proof that a substantial part of the earnings gap is caused by employers' discrimination. The dual labor market excludes women from good jobs and crowds them into jobs that are undervalued and underpaid. Correcting imperfections in the market is necessary but not sufficient. As a remedy, it is upside down: the longer a woman has worked and the more discrimination she has suffered, the less likely she is to benefit.

Second, part of the earnings gap results from sexist socialization that occurs outside the labor market, but this fact is not a reason to let employers go free. Society is a system, and each part connects with every other part.

Women stay home to rear children because women's work is paid so little. Women's work is paid so little because women have no marketable skills. Women have no marketable skills because they stay home to rear children. The vicious circle has to be broken somehow, and with more and more women entering the labor force, comparable worth is an effective way to do it.

Third, job evaluation may not reveal the inherent value of jobs, but it can measure the relative worth of jobs. Certainly job evaluation is used for that purpose now, but is used unfairly because of biases against women's work. This point makes clear that comparable worth is not merely an interest issue. It is a rights issue when women's work is undervalued because of prejudice built into the system.

Fourth, comparable worth will not cause the government to price and allocate labor. Once the value of women's work is fairly determined, the market can be utilized for these purposes again. Until then, however, the market, which reflects the bias against women, cannot be used as a reference point.

Fifth, Title VII was enacted to overcome employment discrimination, including sex discrimination. If that law is used to protect men against discrimination because of race, religion, and national origin, but not to protect women against sex discrimination, the sexism in our society will be clear for all to see.

And finally, half of all women now work, and more will as time goes on. The labor movement, which has raised the standard of comparable worth, will not let it fall.

MODERATOR   Our advocate and critic have discussed the earnings gap, job evaluation, the social and economic consequences of comparable worth, the law of comparable worth, and the relationship of comparable worth to collective bargaining. Although they have not agreed on any of the issues, perhaps our advocate and critic can agree with a statement of Eleanor Holmes Norton, former chair of the Equal Employment Opportunity Commission:

Comparable worth is the most difficult issue that has arisen under Title VII and ultimately it could have the same impact on the nation as school desegregation did in the 1950s.[134]

Notes

1. Elizabeth Waldman and Beverly J. McEaddy, "Where Women Work— An Analysis by Industry and Occupation," *Monthly Labor Review* 97, 5 (1974): 3.

2. Equal Pay Act of 1963, 29 U.S.C. § 206(d) (1976); Title VII, Civil Rights Act of 1964, 42 U.S.C. § § 2000e-17.

3. U.S., Department of Commerce, Bureau of the Census, "Monthly Income of Families and Persons in the United States, 1978," *Current Population Reports,* series P-60, no. 118. (Washington, D.C., 1980), table 57.

4. Donald J. Treiman and Heidi I. Hartmann, eds. *Women, Work, and Wages: Equal Pay for Jobs of Equal Value* (Washington, D.C.: National Academy Press, 1981), p. 16, table 3.

5. U.S., Bureau of the Census, "Monthly Income of Families and Persons," table 51.

6. U.S. Commission on Civil Rights, *Social Indicators of Equality for Minorities and Women* (Washington, D.C., 1978), p. 54, table 4.3.

7. U.S., Department of Labor, Bureau of Labor Statistics, "Women in the Labor Force: Some New Data Series," Report 575 (Washington, D.C., 1979), pp. 1–4.

8. U.S. Commission on Civil Rights, *Social Indicators of Equality,* pp. 56–60.

9. U.S., Department of Labor, Bureau of Labor Statistics, *Handbook of Labor Statistics,* Bulletin no. 2070 (Washington, D.C., 1980), table 22.

10. U.S., Department of Commerce, Bureau of the Census, *Occupational Characteristics,* Census of Population: 1973, Subject Reports PC(2)-7A (Washington, D.C., 1973), table 24.

11. U.S., Department of Labor, Women's Bureau, *Handbook on Women Workers* (Washington, D.C., 1975), pp. 89–91.

12. Hilda Kahne and Andrew I. Kohen, "Economic Perspectives on the Role of Women in the American Economy," *Journal of Economic Literature* 13, 4 (1975): 1249.

13. Treiman and Hartmann, *Women, Work, and Wages,* pp. 28–30, 38.

14. A summary of studies may be found in Treiman and Hartmann, *Women, Work, and Wages,* p. 36.

15. U.S., Bureau of the Census, *Occupational Characteristics,* table 1.

16. John E. Buckley, "Pay Differences between Men and Women in the Same Job," *Monthly Labor Review* 94, 11 (1971): 36.

17. Ronald G. Ehrenberg and Robert S. Smith, *Modern Labor Economics: Theory and Public Policy* (Glenview, Ill.: Scott, Foresman and Co., 1982), pp. 396–97; Treiman and Hartmann, *Women, Work, and Wages,* pp. 53–54.

18. Treiman and Hartmann, *Women, Work, and Wages,* pp. 53–56.

19. On the education factor, U.S., Bureau of the Census, "Monthly Income of Families and Persons," table 51; on the experience factor, Treiman and Hartmann, *Women, Work, and Wages,* p. 23.

20. See Barbara Bergmann, "The Effects of White Incomes on Discrimination in Employment," *Journal of Political Economy* 79 (1971): 294; and "Occupational Segregation, Wages, and Profits When Employers Discriminate by Race or Sex," *Eastern Economic Journal* 1 (1974): 103.

21. U.S., Department of Labor, Bureau of Labor Statistics, *Employment and Earnings* (Washington, D.C., January 1982), p. 65.

22. U.S., Department of Labor, Women's Bureau, *The Earnings Gap between Women and Men* (Washington, D.C., 1979), p. 17.

23. Title VII, § 701(b), 42 U.S.C. 2000e(b).

24. On the appointment of women to professorships, see, e.g., *Sweeney* v. *Board of Trustees of Keene State College,* 604 F.2d 106 (1st Cir. 1979), *cert. denied,* 444 U.S. 1045 (1980); for a discussion of the relative salaries of male and female academics, see Marianne A. Ferber and Carole A. Green, "Traditional or Reverse Sex Discrimination? A Case Study of a Large Public University," *Industrial and Labor Relations Review* 35, 4 (1982); on the employment of women as fire fighters and police officers, see, e.g., *U.S.* v. *City of Chicago,* 549 F.2d 415 (7th Cir. 1977); and on job segregation in factories, see, e.g., *Palmer* v. *General Mills,* 513 F.2d 1040 (6th Cir. 1975).

25. U.S., Department of Labor, Women's Bureau, *Summary of State Laws for Women* (Washington, D.C., 1969).

26. *Phillips* v. *Martin Marietta,* 400 U.S. 542 (1971).

27. *Sprogis* v. *United Air Lines,* 444 F.2d 1194 (7th Cir. 1971), *cert. denied,* 404 U.S. 991 (1971), involved discharge upon marriage; and in *Condit*

v. *United Air Lines,* 558 F.2d 1176 (4th Cir. 1977), the issue was discharge on account of pregnancy.

28. See, e.g., *Rosenfeld* v. *Southern Pacific,* 444 F.2d 1219 (9th Cir. 1971).

29. *Dothard* v. *Rawlinson,* 433 U.S. 321 (1977).

30. Ruth G. Blumrosen, "Wage Discrimination, Job Segregation, and Title VII of the Civil Rights Act of 1964," *University of Michigan Journal of Law Reform* 12 (1979): 423, 444–45.

31. Burton G. Malkiel and Judith A. Malkiel, "Male-Female Pay Differentials in Professional Employment," *American Economic Review* 63, 4 (1973): 693; Charles Nicholas Halaby, "Sexual Inequality in the Workplace: An Employer-specific Analysis of Pay Differences," *Social Science Research* 8, 1 (1979): 79.

32. Joan Talbert and Christine E. Bose, "Wage Attainment Process: The Retail Clerk Case," *American Journal of Sociology* 83, 2 (1977): 403.

33. Ehrenberg and Smith, *Modern Labor Economics,* p. 403.

34. Treiman and Hartmann, *Women, Work, and Wages,* pp. 47–52.

35. Blumrosen, "Wage Discrimination and Title VII," p. 451.

36. See Peter B. Doeringer and Michael J. Piore, *Internal Labor Markets and Manpower Analysis* (Lexington, Mass.: D. C. Heath and Co., 1971).

37. Treiman and Hartmann, *Women, Work, and Wages,* pp. 47–52; see Doeringer and Piore, *Internal Labor Market.*

38. John Kenneth Galbraith, *Economics and Public Purpose* (Boston: Houghton Mifflin, 1973), p. 43.

39. Treiman and Hartmann, *Women, Work, and Wages,* pp. 47–52.

40. Ibid., pp. 66–67.

41. Blumrosen, "Wage Discrimination and Title VII," p. 491.

42. Ehrenberg and Smith, *Modern Labor Economics,* pp. 401–4; see Gary S. Becker, *The Economics of Discrimination,* 2d ed. (Chicago: University of Chicago Press, 1971).

43. Treiman and Hartmann, *Women, Work, and Wages,* pp. 47–48, 64; Ehrenberg and Smith, *Modern Labor Economics,* pp. 406–9; see Edmund S. Phelps, "The Statistical Theory of Racism and Sexism," *American Economics Review* 62 (1972): 659; Blumrosen, pp. 452–53.

44. Mary Hamblin and Michael S. Prell, "The Income of Men and Women: Why Do They Differ?" *Federal Reserve Bank of Kansas City Monthly Review,* April 1963.

45. 400 U.S. 542 (1971).

46. 435 U.S. 702 (1978).

47. Blumrosen, "Wage Discrimination and Title VII," p. 448.

48. Ehrenberg and Smith, *Modern Labor Economics*, pp. 405–6; ibid., see p. 410.

49. Kahne and Kohen, "Economic Perspectives on the Role of Women," p. 1261.

50. Blumrosen, "Wage Discrimination and Title VII," p. 427.

51. U.S. Commission on Civil Rights, *Social Indicators of Equality*, p. 7.

52. See, e.g., *Hodgson* v. *Brookhaven General Hospital*, 436 F.2d 719 (1970).

53. U.S., Bureau of the Census, *Occupational Characteristics*, table 24.

54. Francine D. Blau, *Equal Pay in the Office* (Lexington, Mass.: Lexington Books, 1977).

55. Blumrosen, "Wage Discrimination and Title VII," p. 453; Treiman and Hartmann, *Women, Work, and Wages*, pp. 40–41.

56. Blumrosen, "Wage Discrimination and Title VII," pp. 438–39.

57. Robert G. Storey, "USSR People's Court and Women Lawyers," 48 Women Lawyers' Journal 21 (1962); Blumrosen, "Wage Discrimination and Title VII," p. 408.

58. Blau, *Equal Pay in the Office*; Buckley, "Pay Differences in the Same Job"; Donald J. McNulty, "Difference in Pay between Men and Women Workers," *Monthly Labor Review* 90, 12 (1967): 40.

59. 28 War Labor Reports 666 (1945).

60. 452 U.S. 161 (1981).

61. Bureau of National Affairs, *The Comparable Worth Issue*, BNA Special Report (Washington, D.C.: Bureau of National Affairs, 1981), pp. 29–32.

62. Paula England, Marilyn Chasie, and Linda McCormack, "Skill Demands and Earnings in Male and Female Occupations," *Sociology and Social Research* 66, 2 (January 1982).

63. Paula England, "Do Men's Jobs Require More Skill than Women's?" *ILR Report* (Ithaca, N.Y.: New York State School of Industrial and Labor Relations, Cornell University, Spring 1982), p. 23.

64. Treiman and Hartmann, *Women, Work, and Wages*, pp. 17–24.

65. Andrew I. Kohen, with Susan C. Breinich and Patricia M. Shields, *Women and the Economy: A Bibliography and a Review of the Literature on Sex Differentiation in the Labor Market* (Columbus, Ohio: Center for Human Resource Research, College of Administration, Ohio State University, 1977); Mary Corcoran and Greg J. Duncan, "Work History, Labor Force Attachment, and Earnings Differences between the Races and Sexes," *Journal*

of Human Resources 14, 1 (1979): 3; Treiman and Hartmann, *Women, Work, and Wages*, pp. 19–24.

66. Treiman and Hartmann, *Women, Work, and Wages*, p. 19.

67. Blumrosen, "Wage Discrimination and Title VII," p. 451.

68. Treiman and Hartmann, *Women, Work, and Wages*, pp. 18–24.

69. Ehrenberg and Smith, *Modern Labor Economics*, pp. 397–98.

70. Ehrenberg and Smith, *Modern Labor Economics*, p. 398.

71. U.S., Bureau of Labor Statistics, *Handbook of Labor Statistics*, table 60.

72. Ehrenberg and Smith, *Modern Labor Economics*, p. 398.

73. Blumrosen, "Wage Discrimination and Title VII," pp. 444–45.

74. The example is from Kate Millett, *Sexual Politics* (Garden City, N.Y.: Doubleday and Co., 1970), p. 7; see also Blumrosen, "Wage Discrimination and Title VII," p. 416.

75. Donald J. Treiman, *Occupational Prestige in Comparative Perspective* (New York: Academic Press, 1977), p. 108.

76. These descriptions draw heavily on Donald J. Treiman, *Job Evaluation: An Analytic Review* (Washington, D.C.: National Academy of Sciences, 1979), pp. 1–7.

77. Blumrosen, "Wage Discrimination and Title VII," pp. 435–37; Treiman, *Job Evaluation*, pp. 39–40.

78. Treiman, *Job Evaluation*, pp. 31–38.

79. See Blumrosen, "Wage Discrimination and Title VII," p. 417 n.90, p. 418 n.91, p. 420 n.100.

80. L. S. Fidell, "Empirical Verification of Sex Discrimination in Hiring Practices in Psychology," *American Psychologist* 25, 12 (December 1970): 1094.

81. Benson Rosen and Thomas H. Jardee, "Influence of Sex Role Stereotypes on Personnel Decisions," *Journal of Applied Psychology* 59 (1974): 9.

82. Bureau of National Affairs, *The Comparable Worth Issue*, pp. 29–33.

83. Robert Grams and Donald P. Schwab, "An Experimental Investigation of Evaluation Biases That May Influence Female Job Salaries," working paper (Madison, Wis.: University of Wisconsin, 1982).

84. 499 F. Supp. 1147 (D. D.C. 1980).

85. Treiman, *Job Evaluation*, p. 46.

86. Treiman and Hartmann, *Women, Work, and Wages*, p. 80.

87. George Hildebrand, "The Market System," and Schwab, "Job Evalua-

tion and Pay Setting: Concepts and Practices," both in *Comparable Worth: Issues and Alternatives,* edited by E. Robert Livernash (Washington, D.C.: Equal Employment Advisory Council, 1980), pp. 62–67, 88–93.

88. Blumrosen, "Wage Discrimination and Title VII," pp. 439–40.

89. Hildebrand, "The Market System," pp. 102–6.

90. Adam Smith, *An Inquiry into the Nature and Causes of the Wealth of Nations,* edited by Edwin Cannan, vol. 1 (London: Methuen and Co., 1950), p. 30.

91. R. G. Gregory and R. C. Duncan, "The Relevance of Segmented Labor Market Theories: The Australian Experience of the Achievement of Equal Pay for Women," *Journal of Post Keynesian Economics* 3, 3: 403.

92. Robert Williams and Douglas McDowell, "The Legal Framework," in *Comparable Worth: Issues and Alternatives,* edited by E. Robert Livernash (Washington, D.C.: Equal Employment Advisory Council, 1980), pp. 213–16.

93. 109 Congressional Record 9197.

94. See, e.g., *Angelo* v. *Bacharach Instrument Co.,* 555 F.2d 1164 (3d Cir. 1977), and Williams and McDowell, "The Legal Framework," pp. 232–35.

95. 28 War Labor Reports 666 (1945).

96. 28 War Labor Reports at 670.

97. 28 War Labor Reports at 671.

98. See, e.g., *General Electric and Westinghouse,* 28 War Labor Reports 666, 691 (1945).

99. See, e.g., *Bendix Aviation,* 11 War Labor Reports 669 (1943).

100. See, e.g., *Schultz* v. *Wheaton Glass Co.,* 421 F.2d 259 (3d Cir.), *cert. denied,* 398 U.S. 905 (1970).

101. 436 F.2d 719 (5th Cir. 1970); id. at 725 (footnote omitted).

102. 421 F.2d 259 (3d Cir.), *cert. denied,* 398 U.S. 905 (1970).

103. 451 F. Supp. 967 (W.D. Pa. 1978).

104. 110 Congressional Record 7217.

105. 110 Congressional Record 13,647.

106. Id.

107. 110 Congressional Record 15,896.

108. 452 U.S. 161 (1981). For the specific passages quoted, see, respectively, pages 178, 166 n.8, 166, 181.

109. 620 F.2d 228, 229 (10th Cir.), *cert. denied,* 449 U.S. 888 (1980).

110. 563 F.2d at 355 (8th Cir. 1977) (footnotes omitted).

111. 602 F.2d 882 (9th Cir. 1979), *reh'g denied,* 623 F.2d 1303, 1317, 1321 (1980), *aff'd,* 452 U.S. 161 (1981).

112. 631 F.2d 1094, 1097 (3d Cir. 1980), *cert. denied,* 452 U.S. 967 (1981).

113. 435 U.S. 702, 709 (1978).

114. Michael Evan Gold, "A Tale of Two Amendments: The Reasons Congress Added Sex to Title VII and Their Implication for the Issue of Comparable Worth," 19 *Duquesne Law Review* 467 (1981).

115. 452 U.S. 161, 170, 171 (1981).

116. Id. at 178, 180 (citation omitted).

117. 28 BNA Fair Empl. Prac. Cas. 739, 745 (W.D. Wis. 1982).

118. Blumrosen, "Wage Discrimination and Title VII."

119. 28 BNA Fair Empl. Prac. Cas. 746.

120. 28 BNA Fair Empl. Prac. Cas. 750.

121. Bureau of National Affairs, *The Comparable Worth Issue,* pp. 27–29.

122. Section 105A, Ch. 149, General Laws of Mass., as amended by Ch. 131, L. 1980.

123. Section 337.423, Ch. 114, L. 1966.

124. C. Vann Woodward, *The Strange Career of Jim Crow,* 2d rev. ed. (New York: Oxford University Press, 1966), pp. 82–85, 97–105, 139.

125. Joy Ann Grune, *Manual on Pay Equity: Raising Wages for Women's Work* (Washington, D.C.: Committee on Pay Equity, Conference on Alternative State and Local Policies, 1980), pp. 139–40.

126. Bureau of National Affairs, *The Comparable Worth Issue,* p. 132.

127. Grune, *Manual on Pay Equity,* p. 141.

128. Bureau of National Affairs, *Daily Labor Report,* July 6, 1982, p. A-3; July 7, 1982, p. A-13; July 10, 1982, p. A-4; July 13, 1982, pp. A-3, 4; July 14, 1982, pp. 8, 9.

129. Grune, *Manual on Pay Equity,* pp. 155, 156, 163.

130. *Daily Labor Report,* issues and pages as cited in note 128.

131. U.S., Department of Labor, Bureau of Labor Statistics, *Directory of National Unions and Employee Associations, 1979,* Bulletin no. 2079 (Washington, D.C., 1980), tables 9, 11, appendix E.

132. Virginia A. Bergquist, "Women's Participation in Labor Organizations," *Monthly Labor Review* 97, 10 (October 1974), p. 5.

133. U.S., Bureau of Labor Statistics, *Directory of National Unions,* pp. 62, 63, table 11.

134. Bureau of National Affairs, FEP Summary of Latest Developments No. 383, November 8, 1979.

References

Becker, Gary S. *The Economics of Discrimination.* 2d ed. Chicago: University of Chicago Press (1971).

Bergmann, Barbara. "The Effects of White Incomes on Discrimination in Employment." *Journal of Political Economy* 79 (1971): 294.

———. "Occupational Segregation, Wages and Profits When Employers Discriminate by Race or Sex." *Eastern Economic Journal* 1 (1974): 103.

Bergquist, Virginia A. "Women's Participation in Labor Organizations." *Monthly Labor Review* 97, 10 (October 1974).

Blau, Francine D. *Equal Pay in the Office.* Lexington, Mass.: Lexington Books (1977).

Blumrosen, Ruth G. "Wage Discrimination, Job Segregation, and Title VII of the Civil Rights Act of 1964." *University of Michigan Journal of Law Reform* 12 (1979): 397.

Buckley, John E. "Pay Differences between Men and Women in the Same Job." *Monthly Labor Review* 94, 11 (1971): 36.

Bureau of National Affairs. *The Comparable Worth Issue.* BNA Special Report. Washington, D.C.: Bureau of National Affairs (1981).

———. *Daily Labor Reporter,* July 6, 1982; July 7, 1982; July 10, 1982; July 13, 1982; July 14, 1982.

Corcoran, Mary, and Duncan, Greg J. "Work History, Labor Force

Attachment, and Earnings Differences between the Races and Sexes." *Journal of Human Resources* 14, 1 (1979): 3.

Doeringer, Peter B., and Piore, Michael J. *Internal Labor Markets and Manpower Analysis.* Lexington, Mass.: D. C. Heath and Co. (1971).

Ehrenberg, Ronald G., and Smith, Robert S. *Modern Labor Economics: Theory and Public Policy.* Glenview, Ill.: Scott, Foresman and Co. (1982).

England, Paula. "Do Men's Jobs Require More Skill than Women's?" *ILR Report.* Ithaca, N.Y.: New York State School of Industrial and Labor Relations, Cornell University (Spring 1982).

England, Paula, Chasie, Marilyn, and McCormack, Linda. "Skill Demands and Earnings in Female and Male Occupations." *Sociology and Social Research* 66, 2 (January 1982).

Ferber, Marianne A., and Green, Carole A. "Traditional or Reverse Sex Discrimination? A Case Study of a Large Public University." *Industrial and Labor Relations Review* 35, 4 (1982).

Fidell, L. S. "Empirical Verification of Sex Discrimination in Hiring Practices in Psychology." *American Psychologist* 25, 12 (December 1970): 1094.

Galbraith, John Kenneth. *Economics and the Public Purpose.* Boston: Houghton Mifflin (1973).

Gold, Michael Evan. "A Tale of Two Amendments: The Reasons Congress Added Sex to Title VII and Their Implication for the Issue of Comparable Worth." 19 *Duquesne Law Review* 467 (1981).

Grams, Robert, and Schwab, Donald P. "An Experimental Investigation of Evaluation Biases That May Influence Female Job Salaries." Working paper. Madison, Wis.: University of Wisconsin, 1982.

Gregory, R. G., and Duncan, R. C. "The Relevance of Segmented Labor Market Theories: The Australian Experience of the Achievement of Equal Pay for Women." *Journal of Post Keynesian Economics* 3, 3: 403.

Grune, Joy Ann. *Manual on Pay Equity: Raising Wages for Women's*

Work. Washington, D.C.: Committee on Pay Equity, Conference on Alternative State and Local Policies (1980).

Halaby, Charles Nicholas. "Sexual Inequality in the Workplace: An Employer-specific Analysis of Pay Differences." *Social Science Research* 8, 1 (1979): 79.

Hamblin, Mary, and Prell, Michael J. "The Income of Men and Women: Why Do They Differ?" *Federal Reserve Bank of Kansas City Monthly Review,* April 1973.

Hildebrand, George. "The Market System." In *Comparable Worth: Issues and Alternatives,* edited by E. Robert Livernash. Washington, D.C.: Equal Employment Advisory Council (1980), p. 79.

Kahne, Hilda, and Kohen, Andrew I. "Economic Perspectives on the Role of Women in the American Economy." *Journal of Economic Literature* 13, 4 (1975): 1249.

Kohen, Andrew I., with Breinich, Susan C., and Shields, Patricia M. *Women and the Economy: A Bibliography and a Review of the Literature on Sex Differentiation in the Labor Market.* Columbus, Ohio: Center for Human Resource Research, College of Administration, Ohio State University (1977).

McNulty, Donald J. "Differences in Pay between Men and Women Workers." *Monthly Labor Review* 90, 12 (1967): 40.

Malkiel, Burton G., and Malkiel, Judith A. "Male-Female Pay Differentials in Professional Employment." *American Economic Review* 63, 4 (1973): 693.

Millett, Kate. *Sexual Politics.* Garden City, N.Y.: Doubleday and Co. (1970).

Phelps, Edmund S. "The Statistical Theory of Racism and Sexism." *American Economic Review* 62 (1972): 659.

Rosen, Benson, and Jardee, Thomas H. "Influence of Sex Role Stereotypes on Personnel Decisions." *Journal of Applied Psychology* 59 (1974): 9.

Schwab, Donald. "Job Evaluation and Pay Setting: Concepts and Practices." In *Comparable Worth: Issues and Alternatives,* edited by E. Robert Livernash. Washington, D.C.: Equal Employment Advisory Council (1980).

Smith, Adam. *An Inquiry into the Nature and Causes of the Wealth of Nations*. Edited by Edwin Cannan. Vol. 1. London: Methuen and Co., 1950.

Storey, Robert G. "USSR People's Court and Women Lawyers." 48 Women Lawyers' Journal 21 (1962).

Talbert, Joan, and Bose, Christine E. "Wage Attainment Process: The Retail Clerk Case." *American Journal of Sociology* 83, 2 (1977): 403.

Treiman, Donald J. *Job Evaluation: An Analytic Review*. Washington, D.C.: National Academy of Sciences (1979).
———. *Occupational Prestige in Comparative Perspective*. New York: Academic Press (1977).

Treiman, Donald J., and Hartmann, Heidi I., eds. *Women, Work, and Wages: Equal Pay for Jobs of Equal Value*. Washington, D.C.: National Academy Press (1981).

U.S. Commission on Civil Rights. *Social Indicators of Equality for Minorities and Women*. Washington, D.C. (1978).
———. *Women and Poverty*. Washington, D.C. (1974).

U.S., Department of Commerce, Bureau of the Census. *Occupational Characteristics*. Census of Population: 1970. Subject Reports, Final Report PC(2)-7A. Washington, D.C. (1973).
———. "Monthly Income of Families and Persons in the United States, 1978." *Current Population Reports*, series P-60, no. 118. Washington, D.C. (1980).

U.S., Department of Labor, Bureau of Labor Statistics. *Directory of National Unions and Employee Associations, 1979*, Bulletin no. 2079. Washington, D.C. (1980).
———. *Employment and Earnings*. Washington, D.C. (January 1980).
———. *Employment and Earnings*. Washington, D.C. (January 1982).
———. *Handbook of Labor Statistics*. Bulletin no. 2070. Washington, D.C. (1980).
———. "Women in the Labor Force: Some New Data Series 1–4." Report 575. Washington, D.C. (1979).

U.S., Department of Labor, Women's Bureau. *The Earnings Gap between Women and Men*. Washington, D.C. (1979).

————. *Handbook on Women Workers.* Washington, D.C. (1975).

————. *Summary of State Labor Laws for Women.* Washington, D.C. (1969).

Waldman, Elizabeth, and McEaddy, Beverly J. "Where Women Work—An Analysis by Industry and Occupation." *Monthly Labor Review* 97, 5 (1974): 3.

Williams, Robert, and McDowell, Douglas. "The Legal Framework." In *Comparable Worth: Issues and Alternatives,* edited by E. Robert Livernash. Washington, D.C.: Equal Employment Advisory Council (1980).

Woodward, C. Vann. *The Strange Career of Jim Crow.* 2d rev. ed. New York: Oxford University Press (1966).

Some General Readings

Ruth G. Blumrosen, "Wage Discrimination, Job Segregation, and Title VII of the Civil Rights Act of 1964," 12 *University of Michigan Journal of Law Reform* 399, reviews a wide variety of social science literature and argues that women and blacks can prove a violation of Title VII by proving occupational segregation. A point-by-point reply is Bruce A. Nelson, Edward M. Opton, and Thomas E. Wilson, "Wage Discrimination and the 'Comparable Worth' Theory in Perspective," 13 *University of Michigan Journal of Law Reform* 233.

On job evaluation, see Donald J. Treiman, *Job Evaluation: An Analytic Review* (1979), the interim report to the Equal Employment Opportunity Commission by the National Academy of Sciences, Washington, D.C.

Donald J. Treiman and Heidi I. Hartmann, *Women, Work, and Wages: Equal Pay for Jobs of Equal Value,* the National Academy of Sciences' final report to the EEOC (Washington, D.C.: National Academy Press, 1977) reviews a wide range of social science literature and argues that job evaluation can be used, or reformed, to eliminate sex discrimination in compensation.

Comparable Worth: Issues and Alternatives, edited by E. Robert Livernash (Washington, D.C.: Equal Employment Advisory Council, 1980), contains a collection of essays by leading experts who are critical of comparable worth.

Appendix:
Pertinent Legislation

THE EQUAL PAY ACT OF 1963
29 U.S.C. § 206(d)

The Equal Pay Act amended the Fair Labor Standards Act, 29 U.S.C. § 206(d) to require equal pay for equal work. The relevant subsection of the Fair Labor Standards Act is printed below.

No employer having employees subject to any provisions of this section shall discriminate, within any establishment in which such employees are employed, between employees on the basis of sex by paying wages to employees in such establishment at a rate less than the rate at which he pays wages to employees of the opposite sex in such establishment for equal work on jobs the performance of which requires equal skill, effort, and responsibility, and which are performed under similar working conditions, except where such payment is made pursuant to (i) a seniority system; (ii) a merit system; (iii) a system which measures earnings by quantity or quality of production; or (iv) a differential based on any other factor other than sex: *Provided,* That an employer who is paying a wage rate differential in violation of this subsection shall not, in order to comply with the provisions of this subsection, reduce the wage rate of any employee.

Excerpts from Title VII
of the Civil Rights Act of 1964
The Definitions of Discrimination,
42 U.S.C. § 2000e-2(a)

It shall be an unlawful employment practice for an employer—

(1) to fail or refuse to hire or to discharge any individual, or otherwise to discriminate against any individual with respect to his compensation, terms, conditions, or privileges of employment, because of such individual's race, color, religion, sex, or national origin; or

(2) to limit, segregate, or classify his employees in any way which would deprive or tend to deprive any individual of employment opportunities or otherwise adversely affect his status as an employee, because of such individual's race, color, religion, sex, or national origin.

The Bennett Amendment
42 U.S.C. § 2000e-2(h)

The Bennett Amendment is the second sentence of § 703(h) of Title VII. All of § 703(h), with the Bennett Amendment italicized, is printed below.

Notwithstanding any other provision of this title, it shall not be an unlawful employment practice for an employer to apply different standards of compensation, or different terms, conditions, or privileges of employment pursuant to a bona fide seniority or merit system, or a system which measures earnings by quantity or quality of production or to employees who work in different locations, provided that such differences are not the result of an intention to discriminate because of race, color, religion, sex, or national origin, nor shall it be an unlawful employment practice for an employer to give and to act upon the results of any professionally developed ability test provided that such test, its administration or action upon the results is not designed, intended or used to discriminate because of race, color, religion, sex or national origin. *It shall not be an unlawful employment practice under this title for any employer to differentiate upon the basis of sex in determining the amount of the wages or compensation paid or to be paid to employees of such employer if such differentiation is authorized by the provisions of section 6(d) of the Fair Labor Standards Act of 1938 (29 U.S.C. § 206(d)).*

unfairness given for not for same sex / make identical

job	sex	factor₁	F₂	F₃	F₄	wage
1	1	1	2	4		4
2	1	2	3	6		5
3	1	3	4	8		6
4	1	4	5	10		7
5	1	5	6	12		8
6	2	1	4	2		8
7	2	2	6	3		10
8	2	3	8	4		12
9	2	4	10	5		14
10	2	5	12	6		16

F_2: values ♂ jobs higher
F_3: values ♀ jobs higher
F_4: identical

wage vs. unweighted scores

unweighted values:
7
11
15
19
23

weighted values:
8   9   11
24 14   17 23
28 19 24 29 35